Universal Healthcare

Universal Healthcare

Victoria Sherrow

SERIES EDITOR
Alan Marzilli, M.A., J.D.

CHELSEA HOUSE
PUBLISHERS
An imprint of Infobase Publishing

Chelsea House
An imprint of Infobase Publishing
132 West 31st Street
New York, NY 10001

Library of Congress Cataloging-in-Publication Data

Sherrow, Victoria.
Universal healthcare / Victoria Sherrow.
p. cm. — (Point/counterpoint)
Includes bibliographical references and index.
ISBN 978-1-60413-505-3 (hardcover)
1. Medical policy—United States. 2. Right to health care—United States. 3. Single-
payer health care—United States. 4. Managed care plans (Medical care)—United
States. I. Title. II. Series.

RA395.A3S484 2009
362.1—dc22
                          2009006654

Chelsea House books are available at special discounts when purchased in bulk
quantities for businesses, associations, institutions, or sales promotions. Please call
our Special Sales Department in New York at (212) 967-8800 or (800) 322-8755.

You can find Chelsea House on the World Wide Web at http://www.chelseahouse.com.

Series design by Keith Trego
Cover design by Takeshi Takahashi

Printed in the United States of America

Bang EJB 10 9 8 7 6 5 4 3 2 1

This book is printed on acid-free paper.

All links and Web addresses were checked and verified to be correct at the time of
publication. Because of the dynamic nature of the Web, some addresses and links
may have changed since publication and may no longer be valid.

Alan Marzilli, M.A., J.D.
Birmingham, Alabama

The POINT/COUNTERPOINT series offers the reader a greater understanding of some of the most controversial issues in contemporary
American society—issues such as capital punishment, immigration,
gay rights, and gun control. We have looked for the most contemporary issues and have included topics—such as the controversies
surrounding "blogging"—that we could not have imagined when the
series began.

In each volume, the author has selected an issue of particular
importance and set out some of the key arguments on both sides of the
issue. Why study both sides of the debate? Maybe you have yet to make
up your mind on an issue, and the arguments presented in the book
will help you to form an opinion. More likely, however, you will already
have an opinion on many of the issues covered by the series. There is
always the chance that you will change your opinion after reading the
arguments for the other side. But even if you are firmly committed to
an issue—for example, school prayer or animal rights—reading both
sides of the argument will help you to become a more effective advocate for your cause. By gaining an understanding of opposing arguments, you can develop answers to those arguments.

Perhaps more importantly, listening to the other side sometimes
helps you see your opponent's arguments in a more human way. For
example, Sister Helen Prejean, one of the nation's most visible opponents of capital punishment, has been deeply affected by her interac-
tions with the families of murder victims. By seeing the families' grief
and pain, she understands much better why people support the death
penalty, and she is able to carry out her advocacy with a greater sensi-
tivity to the needs and beliefs of death penalty supporters.

The books in the series include numerous features that help the
reader to gain a greater understanding of the issues. Real-life examples
illustrate the human side of the issues. Each chapter also includes
excerpts from relevant laws, court cases, and other material, which
provide a better foundation for understanding the arguments. The

volumes contain citations to relevant sources of law and information, and an appendix guides the reader through the basics of legal research, both on the Internet and in the library. Today, through free Web sites, it is easy to access legal documents, and these books might give you ideas for your own research.

Studying the issues covered by the POINT/COUNTERPOINT series is more than an academic activity. The issues described in the book affect all of us as citizens. They are the issues that today's leaders debate and tomorrow's leaders will decide. While all of the issues covered in the POINT/COUNTERPOINT series are controversial today, and will remain so for the foreseeable future, it is entirely possible that the reader might one day play a central role in resolving the debate. Today it might seem that some debates—such as capital punishment and abortion—will never be resolved.

However, our nation's history is full of debates that seemed as though they never would be resolved, and many of the issues are now well settled—at least on the surface. In the nineteenth century, abolitionists met with widespread resistance to their efforts to end slavery. Ultimately, the controversy threatened the union, leading to the Civil War between the northern and southern states. Today, while a public debate over the merits of slavery would be unthinkable, racism persists in many aspects of society.

Similarly, today nobody questions women's right to vote. Yet at the beginning of the twentieth century, suffragists fought public battles for women's voting rights, and it was not until the passage of the Nineteenth Amendment in 1920 that the legal right of women to vote was established nationwide.

What makes an issue controversial? Often, controversies arise when most people agree that there is a problem but disagree about the best way to solve it. There is little argument that poverty is a major problem in the United States, especially in inner cities and rural areas. Yet, people disagree vehemently about the best way to address the problem. To some, the answer is social programs, such as welfare, food stamps, and public housing. However, many argue that such subsidies encourage dependence on government benefits while unfairly penalizing those who work and pay taxes, and that the real solution is to require people to support themselves.

American society is in a constant state of change, and sometimes modern practices clash with what many consider to be "traditional values," which are often rooted in conservative political views or religious beliefs. Many blame high crime rates, and problems such as poverty, illiteracy, and drug use on the breakdown of the traditional family structure of a married mother and father raising their children. Since the "sexual revolution" of the 1960s and 1970s, sparked in part by the widespread availability of the birth control pill, marriage rates have declined, and the number of children born outside of marriage has increased. The sexual revolution led to controversies over birth control, sex education, and other issues, most prominently abortion. Similarly, the gay rights movement has been challenged as a threat to traditional values. While many gay men and lesbians want to have the same right to marry and raise families as heterosexuals, many politicians and others have challenged gay marriage and adoption as a threat to American society.

Sometimes, new technology raises issues that we have never faced before, and society disagrees about the best solution. Are people free to swap music online, or does this violate the copyright laws that protect songwriters and musicians' ownership of the music that they create? Should scientists use "genetic engineering" to create new crops that are resistant to disease and pests and produce more food, or is it too risky to use a laboratory to create plants that nature never intended? Modern medicine has continued to increase the average lifespan—which is now 77 years, up from under 50 years at the beginning of the twentieth century—but many people are now choosing to die in comfort rather than living with painful ailments in their later years. For doctors, this presents an ethical dilemma: should they allow their patients to die? Should they assist patients in ending their own lives painlessly?

Perhaps the most controversial issues are those that implicate a constitutional right. The Bill of Rights—the first 10 Amendments to the U.S. Constitution—spells out some of the most fundamental rights that distinguish our democracy from other nations with fewer freedoms. However, the sparsely worded document is open to interpretation, with each side saying that the Constitution is on their side. The Bill of Rights was meant to protect individual liberties; however, the needs of some individuals clash with society's needs. Thus, the Constitution often serves as a battleground between individuals and government officials seeking to protect society in some way. The First Amendment's guarantee of "freedom of speech" leads to some very difficult questions. Some forms of expression—such as burning an American flag—lead to public outrage, but are protected by the First Amendment. Other types of expression that most people find objectionable—such as child pornography—are not protected by the Constitution. The question is not only where to draw the line, but whether drawing lines around constitutional rights threatens our liberty.

The Bill of Rights raises many other questions about individual rights and societal "good." Is a prayer before a high school football game an "establishment of religion" prohibited by the First Amendment? Does the Second Amendment's promise of "the right to bear arms" include concealed handguns? Does stopping and frisking someone standing on a known drug corner constitute "unreasonable search and seizure" in violation of the Fourth Amendment? Although the U.S. Supreme Court has the ultimate authority in interpreting the U.S. Constitution, its answers do not always satisfy the public. When a group of nine people—sometimes by a five-to-four vote—makes a decision that affects hundreds of millions of others, public outcry can be expected. For example, the Supreme Court's 1973 ruling in *Roe v. Wade* that abortion is protected by the Constitution did little to quell the debate over abortion.

Whatever the root of the controversy, the books in the POINT/COUNTERPOINT series seek to explain to the reader the origins of the debate, the current state of the law, and the arguments on either side of the debate. Our hope in creating this series is that readers will be better informed about the issues facing not only our politicians, but all of our nation's citizens, and become more actively involved in resolving these debates, as voters, concerned citizens, journalists, or maybe even elected officials.

This volume examines controversies related to healthcare in the United States, which unlike Canada and many European nations, does not have a single healthcare system to which everyone has access. In a 2007 speech to the Families USA conference, then-Senator Barack Obama called for "affordable, universal health care for every single American." A few months into his presidency, however, he angered veterans' groups when word leaked that his administration was considering requiring veterans to use private insurance to pay for ongoing care for combat-related illnesses and injuries. This flap illustrates some of the challenges facing those who wish to reform the U.S. healthcare system. This volume examines two ongoing debates closely related to the question of whether the United States should adopt universal healthcare. First is the philosophical question of whether healthcare should be regarded as a basic human right, or whether medical care, hospitalization, and medications should be regarded as commodities that should be bought and sold according to peoples' ability to pay. Also examined is the practical question of whether managed care—basing care decisions on models that weigh costs against potential benefits—has a legitimate place in healthcare today.

Healthcare in the United States

Healthcare affects everyone in some way, and Americans tend to have high expectations for healthcare services. People look for advanced technology, informed caregivers, effective treatments, safe facilities, and timely service. At the very least, people hope to obtain essential care at an affordable price.

How well is the American healthcare system working? This question sparks heated debates about the ways in which healthcare—the nation's largest industry—is funded and delivered. Many people receive excellent care, and America is known for its fine medical schools and innovative technology and research, but critics note problems in several key areas, including cost, access, quality, and efficiency.

High Costs for Services and Insurance

One major concern is high costs, which in turn can limit access to services. For decades, prices for healthcare services and products have risen much faster than wages and inflation. That means higher health insurance premiums for individuals and for businesses that fund employee health benefits. Between 1999 and 2007, health insurance premiums increased by 114 percent while wages rose just 27 percent.[1] The U.S. census reported that 45.7 million Americans (about 16 percent) were uninsured in 2007.[2] Another 28 million other Americans were classified as underinsured.[3] In 2008, the average cost of a policy for a family of four living outside Boston ranged from $19,757 to $45,166, depending on the scope of the coverage.[4] Across America, large companies, which can strike better deals with insurance companies, were paying average annual premiums of $12,700 for a family of four, with employees contributing about $3,400 of that amount.[5] Employers have shifted these higher costs to employees, in the form of policies that offer less coverage and have higher copayments and annual deductibles.

High healthcare costs strongly impact government, which funds large public-health programs for low-income adults and children, Americans over age 65, military personnel, and veterans. By 2008, about 25 percent of the federal budget went to healthcare, and state governments struggled to pay their share of public-health programs.[6]

Since many low-income people qualify for government aid, uninsured Americans tend to be middle-income citizens, and most of them hold at least one job. Some employers do not provide insurance, and there are employees who cannot afford to pay their share of the premiums. About 60 percent of all Americans relied on employer-sponsored health insurance in 2008, compared to 68.3 percent in 2000.[7] Self-employed people must buy their own insurance, which costs more for individuals than groups. Still other people lose their insurance due to unemployment, divorce, or serious health problems. People who cannot work for health reasons may lose their insurance when they need it most.

Private insurance companies often reject people with preexisting health problems or offer them coverage at much higher prices than they charge people without known risks or costly health histories. One self-employed 52-year-old man in Maryland faced this situation after a heart attack left him with a $17,000 hospital bill and prescriptions that cost $400 a month. His state funds a plan for high-risk people who cannot afford private insurance, but using it would have cost him $4,752 —unaffordable with his annual income of $35,000 and his high medical debts.[8] The Commonwealth Fund Commission on a High Performance Health System has stated that out-of-pocket healthcare expenses should not exceed 10 percent of income, or 5 percent for people with low incomes.[9]

In 2007, 57 million Americans reported having trouble paying medical bills, compared to about 43 million in 2003.[10] About 80 percent of them lived in families where someone was working fulltime, and 42.5 million *did* have health insurance.[11] People who cannot afford their healthcare may lose their savings and their homes or even go bankrupt. The cost of medical treatment has become the number one cause of bankruptcy in the United States—about half of all personal bankruptcies annually.[12] Studies have shown that most of these people were middle-class, 56 percent were homeowners, and 75 percent had insurance when the bankrupting illness began.[13]

Serious and/or long-term conditions can also exhaust insurance benefits when policies set limits (a "cap") on lifetime payouts. People with a spinal injury, cancer, hemophilia, diabetes, or other costly conditions may use up their benefits before they become eligible for Medicare at age 65. An article in the *Wall Street Journal* told the story of 61-year-old James Dawson, who was admitted to a California hospital after a staph infection spread throughout his body. When Dawson left the hospital five months later, he learned that his insurance policy had paid out the maximum lifetime benefits of $1.5 million. Yet he still owed a $1.2 million hospital bill and thousands of dollars in doctor bills. The itemized hospital bill showed high markups on items like stockings and oxygen masks. Hospitals say these markups are necessary to cover their overall costs, because some people do not pay at all, and insurers and government programs aim to pay discounted rates. As a result, says journalist John Carreyrou, "individuals can, with little warning, be left stuck with wildly inflated hospital bills."[14]

People without insurance often forgo checkups, needed care, or medications. In *Denied: The Crisis of America's Uninsured*, Julie Winokur tells the stories of 41 people who endured serious complications and even died after they lost their jobs and health insurance. One man suffered a fatal heart attack when he did not seek treatment for strep throat, and the infection spread. A woman with a brain tumor was denied treatments for 10 months until she went blind and thus qualified for "urgent" care.[15] People risk seizures, asthma attacks, or other problems because they cannot afford prescription drugs.

Costs and Benefits?

The total of private and public spending on healthcare in the United States reached $2.4 trillion in 2007,[16] up from $1.65 trillion in 2003,[17] and $1.2 trillion in 1999.[18] This money went to hospitals, physicians, dentists, nursing homes, home healthcare, medical supplies, over-the-counter and prescription drugs, and the administrative costs of health insurance. The 2007 figure averages out to more than $7,000 per person—about 50 percent more per person than in other comparable nations. It represented 17 percent of America's gross domestic product (GDP), compared to 9.5 percent in France, 9.7 percent in Canada, 10.7 percent in Germany, and 10.9 percent in Switzerland. The average for all industrialized nations was 9.0 percent of GDP.[19] Because other industrialized nations provide universal healthcare, they also cover every citizen with lower overall costs.

Some analysts say the high cost of healthcare in the United States reflects the use of more advanced technologies and intensive treatments for more people, along with increasing rates of chronic diseases (e.g. diabetes, high blood pressure, and coronary artery disease). People also live longer, and older people use a good deal of healthcare, on average. High costs also come from inefficiency, including waste, duplication, unnecessary services,

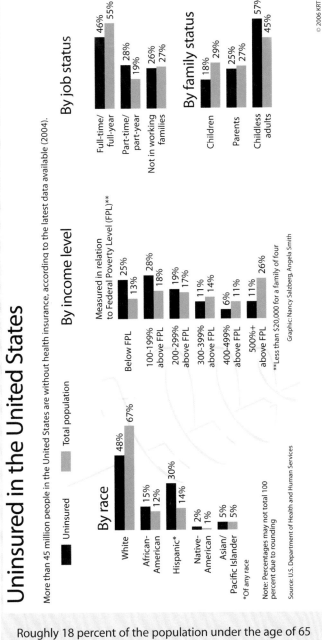

Uninsured in the United States

More than 45 million people in the United States are without health insurance, according to the latest data available (2004).

■ Uninsured ▨ Total population

By race

	Uninsured	Total population
White	48%	67%
African-American	15%	12%
Hispanic*	30%	14%
Native-American	2%	1%
Asian/Pacific Islander	5%	5%

*Of any race

Note: Percentages may not total 100 percent due to rounding

Source: U.S. Department of Health and Human Services

By income level

Measured in relation to Federal Poverty Level (FPL)**

	Uninsured	Total population
Below FPL	25%	13%
100-199% above FPL	28%	18%
200-299% above FPL	19%	17%
300-399% above FPL	11%	14%
400-499% above FPL	6%	11%
500%+ above FPL	11%	26%

**Less than $20,000 for a family of four

Graphic: Nancy Salzberg, Angela Smith

By job status

	Uninsured	Total population
Full-time/full-year	46%	55%
Part-time/part-year	28%	19%
Not in working families	26%	27%

By family status

	Uninsured	Total population
Children	18%	29%
Parents	25%	27%
Childless adults	57%	45%

© 2006 KRT

Roughly 18 percent of the population under the age of 65 lacked health insurance in 2004. The charts seen here break down those numbers by demographics.

and administrative costs. Authors Henry J. Aaron and Joseph P. Newhouse call the way healthcare is financed "uniquely cumbersome and costly . . . a bedlam of uncoordinated payment arrangements" instead of a true "system."[20] Profit margins on products and services, including insurance, nursing home care, and pharmaceuticals, have risen rapidly; starting in the 1980s, the for-profit segment began to account for the biggest growth in the healthcare sector. Critics say that profits enable drug companies to spend about as much on advertising and promotion (about $20 billion a year) as they do on research and development of new drugs.[21]

Does the nation get its money's worth in terms of key health outcomes? Advanced treatments save many lives, and people come from other countries to obtain them. Even so, a report issued in 2008 ranked the United States forty-second in the world in life expectancy—below every country in Western Europe and Scandinavia.[22] The United States ranked nineteenth (last) among industrialized nations in terms of preventing deaths that might not have occurred "with timely and effective health care."[23] It ranked second to last in helping patients coordinate their care and last in assuring that care provided to patients is safe.[24] The infant mortality rate was 7.0 deaths per 1,000 live births, far above the rate of 2.7 in the three countries that rank highest in this area.[25] Dr. Robert H. LeBow says, "Despite our standing as the richest country in the world—and despite our spending nearly twice as much per person on health care than any other country—the overall results have been disappointing, dehumanizing, and at times even abysmal."[26]

The Growth of Healthcare

A brief history of healthcare in America helps to clarify current conditions. Before the twentieth century, healthcare was quite limited. Doctors were called upon to deliver babies, treat wounds, set broken bones, amputate gangrenous limbs, or perform simple surgeries. Many people died young from infectious diseases, incurable conditions, or, for women, in childbirth.

In 1900, Americans had an average life expectancy of 47.3 years, compared to about 78 years today.[27] Hospitals were primarily charitable institutions for poor invalids or the dying.

Scientific research and technology brought better tools for diagnosing and treating illness, easing pain, and performing surgery. By the late 1800s medicine benefited from Pasteur's germ theory, new vaccines, antiseptics for wounds, and Ignaz Semmelweis's crusade to make clean hands standard medical practice during childbirth. X-rays provided inside views of the body for the first time. In 1900, Karl Landsteiner identified three of the four major blood groups, which paved the way for lifesaving transfusions. (The fourth type, AB, was identified by another research team about a year later.) Medicine became more organized, with higher standards for training and licensing physicians, and nursing developed into a respected profession.

As hospitals offered services performed by skilled doctors, nurses, and technicians, they attracted more patients and built new wings and private rooms. By the 1920s, paying patients accounted for more than half of all hospital revenues. About one-third of hospital expenses were paid with donations from religious organizations, philanthropists, and the public. Most hospitals were still nonprofit institutions, and many were run by religious organizations. In some hospitals, training programs for nurses and physicians provided cheap or free labor. Government had a minimal role, though federal and state laws exempted hospitals from certain taxes and made hospital donations tax deductible.

Funds for building and renovating hospitals declined during the 1930s, the time of the Great Depression, and World War II (1939–1945). After the war President Harry S. Truman (1945–53) signed the Hill-Burton Act (Hospital Survey and Construction Act of 1946) to provide federal aid and tax benefits for community hospitals, especially in underserved areas. Hill-Burton was the first major addition to the Public Health Service Act of 1944. In 1954, it funded nursing homes and was used to replace and renovate facilities and add outpatient and rehabilitation services.

In certain poor rural and urban areas, government provided up to 90 percent of the funds for healthcare facilities

The second half of the twentieth century brought significant medical advances, along with more government funding for facilities, including mental health centers. New treatments offered more hope to the mentally ill, and states improved their psychiatric facilities. A growing number of doctors were also specializing in branches of medicine, such as surgery, pediatrics, or psychiatry, instead of choosing general practice. Though healthcare costs kept rising, the U.S. economy was growing during the 1950s and 1960s.

Health Insurance

As healthcare expanded, more people relied on insurance to help pay for treatments and hospitalization. In exchange for a certain amount of money (a premium), the insurer promised to pay certain benefits if the event occurred—in this case illness or accident.

The idea of pooling money to finance health-related expenses was not new. As early as 1798, federal officials levied a tax of 20 cents per sailor on incoming American ships and used this money to build hospitals for seamen in Virginia, Massachusetts, and South Carolina. In 1847, the Health Insurance Company of Philadelphia and the Massachusetts Health Insurance Company of Boston offered the first commercial health insurance policies with comprehensive benefits.[28] By the 1860s, people could buy plans that paid benefits if they were injured during steamboat or rail travel. In the 1870s, mining, railroad, and lumber companies hired company doctors to treat workers. Their salaries came from deducting a fixed amount of money from workers' wages.

At the time, most workers still faced grave problems if they were sick or disabled. Those without savings relied on whatever charity was available. Mutual benefit societies helped to fill that gap by giving people in certain trade groups a small monthly benefit. During the 1860s, groups of silversmiths, watchmakers, and other skilled craftsmen operated "sickness funds." In 1877, the Granite Cutters Union offered members a voluntary insurance plan against illness or injury. This plan failed, but other unions began offering similar plans.

The 1890s saw the creation of group accident and health insurance plans that protected people in the event of fire, flood, theft, and other calamities. Though most individuals do not experience such events, they occur at fairly predictable rates in the general population. By pooling payments from many people, companies "cover" subscribers by using the collected funds to pay those who suffer a loss. By 1911, a hundred of these insurance companies in the United States were focusing solely or mostly on "sickness" or "health" insurance. In 1912, the National Convention of Insurance Commissioners drafted a model states could use to regulate these programs. The next year, the International Ladies Garment Union established the first union-sponsored medical services plan.

Other people wanted similar protection, and hospitals saw health insurance as a way to guarantee a steadier income. In 1929, Baylor University Hospital in Dallas, Texas, contracted with a group of 1,250 teachers to guarantee them a certain number of days in the hospital each year in exchange for a bimonthly fee of 50 cents per person. This plan, named Blue Cross, expanded to include prepayments for possible surgery (Blue Shield). Before long, Blue Cross (for hospitalization) and Blue Shield (for physicians' bills) spread to other states.

By the mid-twentieth century, health insurance was increasingly linked to employment. During World War II, the federal government froze wages, but companies could still offer nonwage benefits to attract scarce labor while many Americans served in the military. After the war, employers continued to offer insurance benefits. By 1950, about half of all Americans had health insurance, primarily hospital coverage.[29] During the next two decades, workplace-based insurance proliferated and plans grew more generous. Labor unions played a key role in gaining these benefits for workers and their families.

Though millions of Americans were covered, millions were not. People lost their coverage if they became self-employed, changed jobs, or retired, usually at age 65. For-profit insurance companies entered the marketplace. The original "Blues" (Blue Cross and Blue Shield) used a system called "community rating." This allows everyone in a given community to pay the same rate for the same insurance package. Other companies realized they could make higher profits by enrolling people who are not likely to get sick. They competed with community-rating plans by offering younger and healthier people cheaper policies (known as "cherry-picking" or "cream-skimming"). This meant even higher costs for companies that continued to cover higher-risk people.

Government Intervention

Early in the 1900s, reformers called for government action, including universal healthcare to help poor working people and the unemployed. Germany had initiated a national program in the nineteenth century, and Great Britain enacted its comprehensive National Insurance Act in 1911. By 1914, 10 European nations had adopted national health plans. The Progressive Party, established by former president Theodore Roosevelt, favored some kind of national health plan in the United States.

As healthcare costs rose, more Americans joined this debate. During the Great Depression, massive unemployment and poverty caused widespread insecurity, especially for the sick, elderly, and disabled. In 1927, a group of concerned physicians, sociologists, public-health experts, economists, and others formed the Committee on the Costs of Medical Care (CCMC). Their final report, issued in 1932, suggested ways to improve the quality of care and provide funding to give all Americans access to health services.

Under President Franklin D. Roosevelt (1933–1945), the Social Security Act of 1935 established a government pension plan for elderly Americans. Roosevelt had also supported a national health insurance component but soon realized Congress would not pass it. The American Medical Association (AMA), founded in 1901, vigorously worked to defeat such a plan. The Social Security Act, however, did offer states grants for funding programs for maternal and child health and crippled children. The Revenue Act of 1939 gave employees tax exemptions for the cost of accident and health insurance.

By 1939, more Americans supported government action. An article in *Consumer Union Reports* said:

There's now no doubt of the growing wave of popular sentiment in favor of an efficient public health program. It has become obvious that the people of the country intend to see that the whole population shall benefit

Committee on the Costs of Medical Care Report of 1932: Majority Recommendations

1. Comprehensive medical service should be provided largely by organized groups of practitioners, organized preferably around hospitals, encouraging high standards and preserving personal relations.

2. All basic public health services should be extended to the entire population, requiring increased financial support, full-time trained health officers and staffs ...

3. Medical costs should be placed on a group payment basis through insurance, taxation, or both ...

4. State and local agencies should be formed to study, evaluate and coordinate services, with special attention to urban-rural coordination.

Source: Joseph S. Ross, "The Committee on the Cost of Medical Care and the History of Health Insurance in the United States." *The Einstein Quarterly of Biology and Medicine*, 2002, p. 131. http://www.aecom.yu.edu/uploadedFiles/EJBM/19Ross129.pdf.

from the discoveries of modern medical science. The only question before the country now is, how soon?[30]

Still, Congress continued to reject national health insurance plans. Opponents said government involvement would limit people's choice of doctor, interfere with personal rights and healthcare decisions, and hurt the quality of care.

Although these debates subsided during World War II, Roosevelt's successor, President Harry S. Truman, promoted a bill that would let citizens buy government health insurance. About half of all Americans had private insurance at the time, and polls taken in 1945 showed that 75 percent supported national insurance.[31] Once again, Republicans, Southern Democrats, business leaders, and organized medicine opposed the plan, calling it "socialist medicine" and "communist."[32] Truman argued that his voluntary plan was not socialistic, but it was defeated.

Government did take some action. Truman appointed the President's Commission on the Health Needs of the Nation (also know as the Magnuson Commission), and the National Institutes of Health were founded in Bethesda, Maryland, based on their suggestion that government fund medical research. To meet the growing need for caregivers, the government funded scholarships and loans for nursing students and aided medical schools. The McCarran-Ferguson Act of 1945 gave the states broad powers to regulate the insurance business but also allowed Congress to pass future laws to regulate this business. Under President Dwight D. Eisenhower (1953–1961), Congress approved the Disability Insurance Program (1954), which added disability benefits to Social Security coverage, as well as the Federal Employees Health Benefits Act (1959).

By the 1960s, about 70 percent of Americans had private health insurance, but that left nearly a third uninsured, and most of them lived below the poverty line. Between 1959 and 1964, poverty rates ranged from 19 to 22.4 percent.[33] Studies in 1963 showed that 54 percent of Americans living in poverty did not see a doctor.[34] The poor included a disproportionate number of minorities, who suffered higher rates of illness and infant mortality and more sick days lost from work than whites. Physicians, nurses, and other healthcare workers were among those who urged government to act.

In his State of the Union Address in 1964, President Lyndon B. Johnson declared a "war on poverty." Johnson's predecessor, John F. Kennedy, had supported a national healthcare plan and said government should at least help people living in poverty and those over age 65, since only half of the elderly had health insurance. Johnson proposed the Medicaid and Medicare programs to fill those gaps. They had public and political support at a time of economic growth and a low federal deficit.

Growing Problems

Medicare and Medicaid were the largest government entitlements since Social Security. Supporters praised them for providing a "safety net" for older Americans and the poor; some even suggested that the government should further reform its "two-tiered" system in which wealthier Americans received better care by guaranteeing universal health insurance. Critics thought otherwise.

QUOTABLE

President Harry S. Truman

On November 19, 1945, President Truman discussed his healthcare initiative in a "Special Message to the Congress Recommending a Comprehensive Health Program":

> Our new Economic Bill of Rights should mean health security for all, regardless of residence, station, or race—everywhere in the United States. We should resolve now that the health of this Nation is a national concern; that financial barriers in the way of attaining health shall be removed; that the health of all its citizens deserves the help of all the Nation.

Source: Alan Derickson, *Health Security for All*. Baltimore: Johns Hopkins University Press, 2005.

They noted the high costs of Medicare and Medicaid and said they represented excessive government involvement. They predicted that these programs would make healthcare costs rise even faster.

Government sought to curb costs, especially during difficult economic times. In 1971, President Richard Nixon (1969–1974) imposed wage and price controls on various sectors in the economy and enforced healthcare cost controls for more than a year after lifting them from other sectors. In 1972, the Professional Standards Review Organizations for Medicare was set up to oversee physicians' treatment choices and the lengths of hospital stays. Government officials and others hoped that "managed care," including health maintenance organizations (HMOs), would curb costs. Unlike traditional insurers, managed care plans take an active role in care decisions. The Federal HMO Act of 1973 gave initial funding for HMOs that met federal standards and required businesses with at least 25 employees to offer an HMO option for health coverage.

Other government actions targeted insurance and health planning. The Employee Retirement Income Security Act of 1974 set standards that employee benefit plans must meet to be tax-exempt. The National Health Planning and Resources Development Act aimed to regulate the growth of hospitals and other facilities, because duplication of services and unused hospital beds can increase cost-per-use.

Before the 1970s, most Americans had employee-based insurance. People did not often change jobs. People over 65 became eligible for Medicare after 1965. With a strong economy, it seemed possible that government could fund health programs without budget deficits. That changed as healthcare costs began to outpace economic growth. During the late twentieth century, medical advances brought more sophisticated and expensive treatments, including medical imagery, coronary bypass, transplants of vital organs, neonatal surgery, in vitro fertilization, microsurgery, and improved kidney dialysis.

With more treatment options, standards for providers also changed. Some doctors felt obliged to order more tests and treatments to avoid lawsuits. By 1984, malpractice premiums reached $2 billion for doctors and at least $1.5 billion for hospitals.[35]

In the 1980s, healthcare became the fastest rising part of the federal budget; the healthcare industry became the nation's second largest employer after education, providing jobs for both skilled and semiskilled labor. Healthcare ranked third in terms of consumer spending, after food and housing.[36] Analysts noted that the use of third-party payers (whether private or public insurance) meant that fewer people paid directly for their care and knew of its cost. In 1960, healthcare spending had totaled $23.6 billion, with 55.5 percent being paid out-of-pocket, 22.9 percent by private third-party payers, 12.7 percent by state and local governments, and 8.9 percent by the federal government.[37] By 1980, with total spending of $217 billion, 27.8 percent was out-of-pocket, 32.1 percent from private third-party payers, and 22.9 percent from the federal government.[38] By 1998, the federal government was paying 33.7 percent, and a growing percentage of each tax dollar went to government health programs.[39]

QUOTABLE

President Lyndon B. Johnson

In his first State of the Union Address, delivered on January 8, 1964, President Johnson declared a "war on poverty" that would, among other initiatives, provide health coverage to the poorest American citizens:

> Many Americans live on the outskirts of hope, some because of their poverty and some because of their color, and all too many because of both. Our task is to help replace their despair with opportunity. This administration today, here and now, declares unconditional war on poverty in America.... The richest nation on earth can afford to win it.... Our chief weapons ... will be better schools, and better health, and better homes, and better training, and better job opportunities to help more Americans.

Source: Lyndon B. Johnson in *State of the Union Addresses*. Whitefish, Mont.: Kessinger Publishing, 2004.

Healthcare costs affect prices for almost everything, since both private businesses and the government offer insurance benefits to employees. To address the lack of insurance caused by job loss, Congress passed the Consolidated Omnibus Budget Reconciliation Act (COBRA) in 1985. It requires companies with at least 20 employees to offer partially subsidized health insurance for up to 18 months to terminated employees and their families. In the 1990s, employers expressed increasing concerns about the cost of insuring workers and retirees. They noted that American goods had trouble competing with goods from countries where manufacturing costs are lower.

By 1992, the healthcare system was said to be in crisis, and Americans listed it as a major concern. Costs were still rising. Managed care plans had succeeded in lowering some costs but were increasingly controversial. President George H.W. Bush (1989-1993) favored small changes that relied on the free market, including tax credits that would help lower-income workers and companies buy health insurance. During the early 1990s, Congress considered, but then defeated, seven major healthcare reform bills.

By 1994, more than 37 million Americans were uninsured, and an additional 20 million were called "underinsured," meaning they had trouble covering high out-of-pocket expenses. When President Bill Clinton took office in 1993, he promised healthcare reform, and First Lady Hillary Rodham Clinton spearheaded efforts to develop a plan to cover all Americans. The resulting bill was a blend of private and public insurance based on the idea of "managed competition." Congress debated the Clinton plan for a year but ultimately rejected it. Major opponents, including private health insurance companies, pharmaceutical companies, small business owners, and the AMA, said the plan was too complex and costly and that it gave government too much control.

As had happened before, Congress approved smaller measures to fill specific gaps. The Mental Health Parity Act of 1996 provides more benefits for mental conditions, because physical problems traditionally received better coverage. The Health Insurance Portability and Accountability Act helps workers carry their insurance from job to job and includes regulations to prevent fraud and abuse. In 1997, Congress passed the State Children's Health Insurance Protection (SCHIP), which covered 11 million uninsured children. More children became eligible in 2006 when enrollment standards were expanded to include families with an income three times the poverty level. In 2003, the government under President George W. Bush (2001–2009) enacted the Medicare Prescription Drug Improvement and Modernization Act, which provides an entitlement benefit for retirees for prescription drugs through subsidies and tax breaks. In February 2009, President Barack Obama signed legislation that reauthorized and expanded SCHIP.

New Calls for Action

At the dawn of the current century, critics cited problems in the healthcare system that had persisted for decades: high costs, lack of universal access, fragmented payment and delivery systems, uneven quality, inefficiency, medical errors, and fraud and abuse. For these problems, critics have blamed hospitals, healthcare providers, pharmaceutical companies, and systems of third-party payment (both private insurance and government). Consumers have been blamed for overusing healthcare services, failing to buy insurance when they can afford it, and not taking enough responsibility for their own health.

Support for reform tends to fluctuate, depending on how strongly people feel about their situation. Concerns have grown recently during the severe economic recession that began in December 2007. With unemployment rising sharply, the number of uninsured Americans under 65 hit new highs. These uninsured people included 11 percent of America's children, or about one in nine. Most of them (88.2 percent) had at least one employed parent and more than 50 percent lived in two-parent households.[40] Businesses and the government faced mounting costs. In 2007, U.S. businesses spent $500 billion in employee and retiree health insurance.[41] That same year, the federal government spent $440 billion for Medicare[42] and federal and state governments spent $333 billion for Medicaid.[43]

Participants in the healthcare system voiced their concerns: For physicians, these concerns included lower fees, high malpractice premiums, large amounts of time spent on record keeping and dealing with payers, and less independence to make decisions with their patients. State and federal government saw huge and unsustainable portions of their budgets going to healthcare. Consumers worried about the costs for insurance and deductibles, loss of insurance, and quality of care. In a 2007 survey, 60 percent of the respondents rated the U.S. healthcare system as "fair" (29 percent) or "poor" (30 percent). Nearly one in four said the system was so flawed that it should be completely overhauled, and 47 percent said it needs "major changes."[44] A survey taken in 2006 found that only 18 percent were satisfied with the cost of their healthcare.[45]

Where does one begin to reform this complicated multi-payer system? As author Laurene Graig points out, "The U.S. health care system has never been easy to explain—witness the terms most commonly used to describe it: complex, uncoordinated, loosely structured, fragmented, nondesigned—and even harder to comprehend."[46]

Critics say that the incentives in the U.S. system are misplaced. Providers are paid for performing services and not for keeping people healthy. When providers are forced to work for little or no fee, they have an incentive to raise fees for other people. Insurance companies have incentives to cover people who will not incur high costs and to deny care when possible, because that boosts profits. Consumers who have excellent insurance benefits have incentives to overuse healthcare services. People without insurance have incentives to avoid routine care, which can lead to worse illnesses that require emergency room treatment—free to them but costly to the system.

At the core of these debates is the role of government and the free market in the healthcare system. People also disagree about how much change is needed. Some want sweeping reforms, such as completely changing the way Americans pay for healthcare to a

What Kind of Healthcare System Might Best Serve Americans?

Healthcare expert Dr. Theodore R. Marmor offers a list of basic areas he thinks reformers must address:

1. Financing. What is required is broad-based financing—spreading the costs of medical care, not concentrating them as we do now on the old, the low-income group, or those without employer-based coverage.

2. Universal eligibility and broad coverage.

3. Tough cost controls that would keep spending in bounds.

4. Rewards for the creation of more efficient groups of providers, who are responsive to patients within the discipline of limited budgets.

5. Measures to simplify insurance for patients, payers, and providers.

6. Institutions of clear accountability for the cost, quality and accessibility of the care provided.

7. Freedom of choice. No reform that ignores professional concerns about autonomy will prove workable. But autonomy need not extend to charging whatever one wishes. No reform that limits patients' choice of doctor is desirable when dictated by financial pressures falling dispro-portionately on less affluent or more sickly Americans.

8. Means of consultation and redress. Measures that regularly and trans-parently express patient and provider concerns, within budget con-straints, are essential.

Source: Theodore R. Marmor, *Understanding Health Care Reform*. New Haven, Conn.: Yale University Press, 1994, pp. 15–17.

government single-payer system, resulting in universal Medicare. Other people want incremental, not major, changes.

Most people agree there is no "perfect" system—all involve trade-offs in terms of cost, access, efficiency, and social equity. Around the world, nations have forged systems that differ in terms of the extent of central control and government regulation, the role of private insurance, and the way costs are shared. These systems reflect diverse national values, political processes, social priorities, and resources.

Summary

Modern healthcare has become increasingly sophisticated and expensive, and insurance has become the main means of paying for routine healthcare. For more than a century, reformers have called for a national health insurance program in the United States, but these efforts have been defeated. Opposition has come from organized medicine, for-profit insurance companies, pharmaceutical corporations, conservative politicians, and Americans who are satisfied with their insurance and/or do not like the idea of more government involvement. Despite this, two single-payer systems, Medicare and Medicaid, became law in 1965, and numerous other government actions have followed.

Healthcare debates have intensified in the twenty-first century as people look to increase access, improve efficiency and effectiveness, and control costs. These debates involve philosophical questions, including the question of whether healthcare is a "right." People also debate the roles of government and the free market, in terms of delivering and paying for healthcare, and the roles and responsibilities of patients, providers, employers, and taxpayers. As the following chapters will show, proposals to achieve universal healthcare reflect diverse moral, ethical, political, and economic views.

Healthcare Is a Basic Human Right

Is universal healthcare a right? Or should we regard it as just another commodity in the marketplace, similar to cars, clothing, or television sets? Around the world, people have considered this question, and dozens of nations have concluded that healthcare is indeed a basic human right by providing universal healthcare for their citizens. The United Nations and other international organizations have also declared that quality healthcare is a right.

In the United States, however, the debate continues. During the 2008 presidential campaign, millions of Americans said affordable healthcare was among their top concerns. On October 6, Senator John McCain and then-Senator Barack Obama met in Nashville, Tennessee, for the second presidential debate. Moderator Tom Brokaw asked the candidates, "Is health care in America a privilege, a right, or a responsibility?" McCain replied,

"I think it's a responsibility. . ." and Obama said, "Well, I think it should be a right for every American."[1]

How a nation answers this question tends to determine how its healthcare system will be organized and funded. People who see healthcare as a right often say government should actively ensure universal healthcare. People who view healthcare as a commodity tend to favor private health plans and free-market approaches in which providers operate for profit with minimal government involvement. A healthcare system based on the idea of rights is more apt to consider how well it provides care, not just its profitability. Norman Daniels writes:

> This principle of justice [a right to healthcare] has implications for both access and resource allocation. It implies that there should be no financial, geographical, or discriminatory barriers to a level of care which pro-motes normal functioning. It also implies that resources be allocated in ways that are effective in promoting normal functioning.[2]

People who say healthcare is a right cite principles of ethics, equality, and social justice, as well as the crucial nature of healthcare in people's lives. They note the serious problems that afflict individuals and society when people cannot get access to healthcare services, and the benefits to all when healthcare is a citizen's right.

Healthcare has a special importance in people's lives because it is vital for human functioning.

Can we equate healthcare with other goods and services? Healthcare is not only different but also more important. It can determine our quality of life and even whether we live or die. Without a decent level of health, people cannot function well in daily life or contribute as much to society. Children in poor health face more challenges in school and are unlikely to reach their potential. Health is more basic to functioning than education, yet public education has long been recognized as a right in the United States, and few people would suggest that government abandon that idea.

In 1983, the President's Commission for the Study of Ethical Problems in Medicine and Biomedical and Behavioral Research, established under President Ronald Reagan (1981–1989), took note of these special features and declared that

> society has an ethical obligation to ensure equitable access to health care for all. This obligation rests on the special importance of health care, which derives from its role in relieving suffering, preventing premature death, restoring functioning, increasing opportunity, providing information about an individual's condition, and giving evidence of mutual empathy and compassion.[3]

International organizations recognize healthcare as a right, and the United States has signed treaties and declarations to that effect.

Since the 1940s, the international community has recognized the right to healthcare in numerous documents and declarations. Organizations that champion this right include the United Nations (UN), the World Health Organization (WHO), the Inter-American Court of Human Rights, and the International Labour Organization (ILO). The United States has signed documents and ratified treaties that identify healthcare as a human right.

The United States helped to draft the United Nation's Universal Declaration of Human Rights (UDHR), which the UN adopted in 1948. Article 25 of the declaration states:

> Everyone has the right to a standard of living adequate for the health and well-being of himself and of his family, including food, clothing, housing and medical care and necessary social services, and the right to security

in the event of unemployment, sickness, disability, widowhood, old age or other lack of livelihood in circumstances beyond his control.[4]

In 1966, the UN General Assembly ratified two new treaties based on the UDHR, thus making them international law. They include the International Covenant on Civil and Political Rights (ICCPR), which the U.S. Senate finally ratified in 1992. Article 6 says in part: "Every human being has the inherent right to life. This right shall be protected by law. No one shall be arbitrarily deprived of his life."[5] In its interpretations of Article 6, the UN Human Rights Committee has said that governments must "adopt positive measures" to protect a right to life—for instance, taking actions to abolish malnutrition and epidemic diseases, reduce infant and maternal mortality, and increase life expectancy.

In October 1977, the United States signed the second offshoot of the 1948 declaration, the International Covenant on Economic, Social, and Cultural Rights (ICESCR), which the General Assembly had ratified a decade earlier, in 1967. One passage declares: "The right of everyone to the enjoyment of the highest available standard of physical and mental health [implemented by] the creation of conditions which would assure to all, medical service and medical attention in the event of sickness."[6]

Nations in various regions, including South America, Africa, Europe, and Southeast Asia, have made agreements that support and broaden the ICESCR. The Organization of American States (OAS) adopted its American Declaration of the Rights and Duties of Man in 1948. Article XI states: "Every person has the right to the preservation of his health through sanitary and social measures relating to food, clothing, housing and medical care, to the extent permitted by public and community resources." In this document, the Right to Health appears before the Right to Education, located in Article XII.[7] In 1984, the Inter-American Court on Human Rights ruled that these rights apply to situations beyond traditional healthcare facilities or services when it told the Brazilian government to take preventive and remedial measures to protect the lives and health of indigenous people during a planned building project.[8]

In 2002, the international community affirmed the right to healthcare when the International Labour Organization (ILO) met in Geneva, Switzerland. The ILO, which sees health as vital for a productive labor force, passed a new Resolution Concerning Health Care as a Basic Human Right.[9]

Other industrialized nations recognize the right to healthcare.

Around the world, industrialized nations have developed universal healthcare programs that reflect the UDHR, the UN Convention on the Rights of the Child (UNCRC), and other

The UN Convention on the Rights of the Child, Article 24

The UN Convention on the Rights of the Child (UNCRC) confirmed a child's right to healthcare. Signing nations agree that children have a right to regular primary healthcare, including preventive care, and to public health education. It states that mothers have the right to access care that can reduce infant mortality. In 1989, every nation in the UN, except Somalia and the United States, signed this convention. In the mid-1990s both of these countries signed the UNCRC. Article 24 of the convention states:

> The child has a right to the highest standard of health and medical care attainable. Nations shall provide special emphasis on the provision of primary and preventive health care, public health education and the reduction of infant mortality. They shall encourage international cooperation in this regard and strive to see that no child is deprived of access to effective health services.

Source: http://www.unhchr.ch/html/menu3/b/k2crc.htm.

international agreements. These nations have made healthcare a constitutional right, and, in 2000, it was written into the European Union Charter of Fundamental Rights. Many nations recognized the right to healthcare decades ago. Examples include Germany (1880s), Switzerland (1911), New Zealand (1941), Australia (1941), Canada (1944), Belgium (1945), Sweden (1947), the United Kingdom (1948), Japan (1958), Denmark (1961), Greece (1961), Portugal (1976), France (1978), Italy (1978), Spain (1978), Taiwan (1995), and South Africa (1996).[10]

The failure to recognize a right to healthcare diminishes America's position as a world leader and champion of human rights. America is the wealthiest nation on earth, yet it is the only industrialized nation where people can become impoverished because of illness or injury.

A right to healthcare reflects American values of equality and justice.

Lack of access to healthcare perpetuates racial and socioeconomic inequities. People who can afford such care are better able to

European Union Charter of Fundamental Rights

According to its Web site, the European Union Charter of Fundamental Rights "sets out in a single text, for the first time in the European Union's history, the whole range of civil, political, economic and social rights of European citizens and all persons resident in the EU." Among these rights is a right to healthcare. Chapter 4, Article 25 of the charter states:

> Everyone has the right of access to preventive health care and the right to benefit from medical treatment under the conditions established by national laws and practices. A high level of human health protection shall be ensured in the definition and implementation of all Union policies and activities.

Source: http://www.europarl.europa.eu/charter/pdf/text_en.pdf.

maintain wealth and move up the economic ladder. Poorer people with unmet healthcare needs or burdensome medical bills fall behind. Dr. Lawrence Schneiderman notes:

> [W]e are seeing the gap widen between people who can afford the fanciest health care who are at the same time draining resources away from the increasing number of people who just need decent health care. . . . this is unconscionable . . . every responsible ethicist I know who has thought about this issue has a similar opinion.[11]

Statistics show wide gaps among groups of people in terms of important health indicators. Minorities are more likely to be uninsured or have minimal coverage. A government report states that in 2005 about 13 percent of white Americans under age 65 lacked health insurance, but those figures were 34 percent and 21 percent, respectively, for Hispanics and blacks.[12] These same minorities have, on average, shorter life spans and higher rates of premature births and infant mortality than whites.[13] A 2008 report showed a 30-year gap in average life expectancy between residents of Mississippi, which ranked last in life expectancy, and the more affluent state of Connecticut, which ranked first. Lack of health insurance was cited as one of the main factors associated with premature death.[14] Noting the disparities among economic and racial groups, the Center for Economic and Social Rights concluded:

> This record can be largely attributed to the notion that health care is simply one commodity among others, a privilege for those who can afford it rather than a fundamental right for all. With a system that values profits over people, it is no surprise that health care costs continue to spiral out of control for ordinary Americans even as HMOs and pharmaceutical companies accumulate record-breaking profits.[15]

People who dispute the right to healthcare claim that no such rights appear in the U.S. Constitution or other laws. Clearly, the nation's founders could not make detailed plans for today's complex society or foresee the immense changes in medical technology. They did, however, envision an egalitarian society with opportunities for all, and the preamble to the Constitution champions the need to "promote the general welfare."

Throughout history, civil rights have expanded along with changing conditions and social awareness. Rights that people now take for granted were once nonexistent. Slavery was legal in the United States until the Thirteenth Amendment to the Constitution was enacted in 1865. Women could not vote before the Nineteenth Amendment was passed in 1920. Before 1964, people could legally be denied housing, jobs, and service in a restaurant because of their skin color. People with disabilities did not gain the right to educational facilities on par with those of the nondisabled until 1990.

The nation has thus adapted to its citizens' changing needs by amending the Constitution and by enacting new laws that benefit "we, the people" and promote opportunity. The President's Commission for the Study of Ethical Problems in Medicine and Biomedical and Behavioral Research noted this "ethical obligation" in 1983 when it said government should make access to healthcare possible through a national policy.[16] U.S. Representative Jesse Jackson Jr. is among those who support a constitutional amendment to mandate universal healthcare. He writes, "What if the Constitution said: 'All citizens shall enjoy the right to health care of equal high quality and the Congress shall have the power to implement this article by appropriate legislation?'"[17]

Most Americans, including leaders in diverse fields, agree that healthcare is a right.

For many decades, prominent individuals and groups, including politicians, the clergy, civil rights leaders, labor organizations, teachers, and healthcare providers, have said healthcare is a right. Recent polls show most Americans agree.

Politicians from different parties have supported healthcare rights. When President Truman proposed his comprehensive health plan in 1945, he spoke of an "Economic Bill of Rights" to ensure "health security for all, regardless of residence, station, or race—everywhere in the United States."[18] When he declared war on poverty, President Lyndon Johnson told Congress all Americans should have access to "the wonders of modern medicine."[19] During hearings on health reform held in 1968, Governor Nelson Rockefeller of New York called healthcare a "basic human right" saying that access to hospital services was necessary for full participation in "the opportunities of American life."[20] In 2007, Governor Arnold Schwarzenegger of California proposed a plan to achieve universal coverage in his state with a plan that would have covered all children, regardless of their immigration status.

Clergy from different denominations have discussed the right to healthcare. The Reverend Martin Luther King Jr., a Baptist minister as well as the premier leader of the civil rights movement, said, "Of all forms of inequality, injustice in health is the most shocking and inhumane."[21] In 1981, the U.S. Conference of Catholic Bishops' Pastoral Letter on Health and Health Care

QUOTABLE

Senator Edward M. ("Ted") Kennedy

Senator Kennedy of Massachusetts has been a universal healthcare advocate since the 1970s. In recent years, he declared:

Health care is not just another commodity. It is not a gift to be rationed based on the ability to pay.

Source: "Challenges at Home and Abroad." Forum series sponsored by the John F. Kennedy Presidential Library and Foundation, April 28, 2002.

Reform stated, "Every person has the right to adequate health care. This right flows from the sanctity of human life and the dignity that belongs to all persons, who are made in the image of God."[22] In its "Faithful Reform in Health Care," this group stated: "Following on these principles and on our belief in health care as a basic human right, we call for the development of a national health insurance program ... that will ensure a basic level of health care for all Americans."[23] In 1997, speaking as a representative of the Union of American Hebrew Congregations and the Central Conference of American Rabbis, Rabbi David Saperstein called healthcare reform "a quintessentially religious issue":

> God did not divide creation between those who are entitled to health care and those who are not. Rather, God created us with equal rights, and charged us to take responsibility for one another. People have always understood the obligation to bring health to all, and healing to the sick and infirm. . . . Jews, Christians and Muslims have all agreed that the question "Am I my brother's keeper?" must be answered in the affirmative.[24]

Imam Sa'dullah Khan, of the Islamic Center of Southern California, has said, "We believe that health is a fundamental human right which has, as its prerequisite, social justice and equality and that it should be equally available and accessible to all."[25]

Groups of physicians and nurses have also called healthcare a right, including the American College of Physicians (ACP), the American Medical Student Association (AMSA), Physicians for a National Health Program (PNHP), and American Nurses Association (ANA). In 1995, the founders of PNHP said, "It is time to establish a right to health care, just as the right to a public education was established two hundred years ago."[26]

Recent surveys show that most Americans agree. In 2004, the group Community Voices: Health Care for the Underserved released the results of a survey conducted by the Opinion Research Corporation in which 77 percent of those Americans polled said that healthcare should be a right.[27] In another survey taken that year, 78 percent answered "yes" when asked: "Should America treat health care like other necessities of life, such as water and electricity, that are regulated by government to ensure fair prices, accountability, access for everyone, and quality services?"[28] In 2007, a nationwide poll conducted among Republican voters (many of whom are generally thought to be against government-run universal healthcare) showed that 51 percent thought universal healthcare should be the right of every American.[29] Seventy-one percent of those polled called themselves "conservatives."[30]

Recognizing the right to healthcare benefits society.

Society sees practical benefits from a healthy citizenry. Larger numbers of productive workers boost the economy, and healthcare can also prevent illnesses and control problems before they worsen and cost much more.

Public-health problems also arise when people lack access to medical care. Those who are not immunized may spread infectious diseases—often across borders. In 2001, Dr. Gro Harlem Brundtland, director-general of the WHO, told an international gathering at the World Economic Forum in Lyons, France:

> In the modern world, bacteria and viruses travel almost as fast as money. With globalization, a single microbial sea washes all of humankind. There are no health sanctuaries. The separation between domestic and international health problems is no longer useful. Millions of people cross international borders every single day. A tenth of humanity each year.[31]

In light of such public health threats, ethicist Larry Churchill observed, "The needs of others are not distant objects of my philanthropy but part of my own security."[32]

What about those who say taxpayers should not bear the cost for universal healthcare? They say this forces taxpayers to participate against their will, which impinges on their freedoms, and that such programs involve an unfair redistribution of wealth. But Americans already pay taxes, and local, state, and federal governments allocate these monies as they see fit. Taxpayers cannot specify where their taxes go—and they are often opposed to using taxpayer monies for certain purposes, such as funding abortions, military spending, or subsidies for tobacco farmers. Some citizens might actually prefer to see their taxes used for healthcare. In his article "Warfare and Healthcare," Norman Solomon pointed out that in March 2008 the United States was spending $2 billion per day on military activities, which included the wars in Iraq and Afghanistan, money that could be used to fund universal healthcare at home.[33]

At any rate, the public already pays for nonpaying patients, through higher insurance rates and inflated bills. Certain state and federal laws, including the Consolidated Omnibus Reconciliation Act of 1985, require hospitals to treat the uninsured and the indigent. To offset those costs, providers set higher fees. Dr. John Kitzhaber, a former physician and two-term governor of Oregon, said, "We do have a de facto policy of universal access: It's called the emergency room. Then those uncompensated costs are shifted back to people who have insurance coverage by increasing their bills or increasing their insurance premiums."[34]

The current system leads to other negative economic outcomes. Women who lack healthcare during pregnancy may suffer complications that cost far more than standard prenatal care, or they may give birth to premature babies that require intensive care. People with high blood pressure may suffer preventable strokes and heart attacks. An abscessed tooth can cause infection throughout the body and even be fatal. In 2007, Mitt Romney, who was then governor of Massachusetts, discussed financial aspects after his state passed a new law that requires all residents to obtain insurance and helps lower-income residents to pay for it. Romney said, "It cost us no more money to help people buy insurance policies that they could afford than it was costing us before, handing out free care."[35]

Opponents claim that declaring healthcare a right is a slippery slope that would require government to guarantee everyone any kind of healthcare another person might obtain. This is untrue, since a nation can provide a decent minimum of basic healthcare without giving people an unlimited, unaffordable entitlement. Economic expert Alain Enthoven makes this very point: "A just and humane society can define a minimum standard of medical care that ought to be available to all its members."[36]

Summary

The right to healthcare is well-established in international agreements and the laws of industrialized nations. It reflects the values embodied in the U.S. Constitution and is, indeed, vital to forming "a more perfect union." Healthcare should not be just a privilege for those who can afford it. Dr. Judyann Bigby notes:

> If health care is not a basic right, it means we are a society that believes that we should allow individuals, including children, the elderly, the disabled and all others to suffer or die when they are sick or injured simply because they cannot pay for effective care or treatment.[37]

Practices in healthcare financing and delivery should reflect a clear focus on the health and wellbeing of all Americans, with a system that values people over profits.

Healthcare Is a Marketplace Commodity That People Can Buy and Sell

The idea that everyone has a "right" to healthcare is unfounded. Healthcare can be more accurately described as a need and as a marketplace commodity. Making healthcare an entitlement places unfair obligations on citizens to provide and fund health-care services for others, primarily strangers; it also diminishes individual rights and the responsibility to provide for one's own needs and care for one's health.

Practical problems also arise when nations endorse a "right" to healthcare. Who will define the boundaries of such a "right" or decide how to implement it? This approach gives government far too much control over people's lives and shifts tax resources to healthcare that can be used in other beneficial areas of the economy. In fact, universal access to healthcare might not even lead to improved health for larger numbers of people.

Healthcare does not meet the criteria of a true right or fits traditional American or constitutional ideas about rights.

As Sheldon Richman says, healthcare can more aptly be called a "pseudoright," meaning "any claim expressed in rights language that would expand the power of the state at the expense of genuine rights."[1] Rights define what Americans can do without interference. The basic idea of liberty is that people can be free from government interference to pursue things they want and need.

The idea that healthcare is a "right" goes against American traditions and the intentions of the nation's founders. Documents that protect our liberties give people the chance to pursue things, not the right to possess the things themselves. Citing the inalienable rights to "life, liberty and the pursuit of happiness" set forth in the Declaration of Independence, Michael Burton suggests:

> Notice that these rights are not goods or services, not housing or healthcare, not education or food. The right to life, for example, does not mean that someone has to provide you with food and water; it means you are free to work to earn your food and water and others may not steal them from you once you have them.[2]

Similarly, Leonard Peikoff notes, "Observe that all legitimate rights have one thing in common: they are rights to action, not to rewards from other people. . . . The system guarantees you the chance to work for what you want—not to be given it without effort by somebody else."[3]

The United States has favored narrower definitions when it comes to rights, choosing instead to emphasize individual freedoms and opportunities, including the opportunity to provide for oneself. Other countries have reached different conclusions, based on their own histories and laws, in deciding that government has a duty to provide entitlements designed to serve the larger public good.[4]

No right to healthcare can be found in the U.S. Constitution or in other laws. In fact, courts have concluded that there is no constitutional right to healthcare. For example, in *Maher v. Roe* (1977), the U.S. Supreme Court found that states are not obliged to fund abortions for women in the Medicaid system. The plaintiff's claim was based, in part, on the Equal Protection Clause of the Fourteenth Amendment to the Constitution. The court ruled that government need not fund nontherapeutic abortions for Medicaid recipients just because it chooses to pay for expenses related to childbirth. The court also said that government does not have a duty to remove any burden that might occur as a result of the unequal distribution of wealth. In its decision, the court declared: "Financial need alone does not identify a suspect class for purposes of equal protection analysis."[5] In *Harris v. McRae* (1980), the Supreme Court noted that its decision in *Roe v. Wade* (1973) permits abortions within certain limits, and so government cannot bar women from obtaining them. This does not require government to pay for abortions, however, since the government did not create the conditions that make it harder for poorer people to buy healthcare. The court therefore upheld the Hyde Amendment, which bans the use of federal Medicaid funds for abortions unless the life or health of the mother is in jeopardy.

Vast entitlements place unreasonable burdens on government and minimize individual responsibility.

The entitlements that flow from a "right" to healthcare trigger numerous social and economic costs. Richard A. Epstein writes:

> We must be careful not to decree legal rights to housing or health care. We must focus more on the flip side of rights: their correlative costs. We must face the

possibility that someone may have to "do without" in a world of scarcity. We can no longer start our public debate with the false but comforting assumption that our social abundance can support social safety nets and minimal entitlements to everyone in society. We can no longer declare that certain rights are "special" and thus immune from critical challenge and review.[6]

Those who support a right to healthcare often say that this stems, in part, from its special importance in people's lives. People need many other things as well. In America, people are free to transact business with other people to acquire things they need, including food, water, shelter, clothing, and healthcare.

Government does not have an obligation, or even the capacity, to fix all social inequalities or provide people with all their needs and wants. Certain broad public-health measures, such as sanitation, pollution control, and laws that protect workers, are justified because individuals cannot control those things on their own. Individuals can and do obtain health insurance and healthcare through their own resources, however, and they are free to do so. Political commentator Scott McPherson remarks:

> It is the responsibility of each and every American to provide for his own medical needs, by contracting for such services on the free and open market. The only effective role Congress or the president can play in any debate about health care is to accept that socialized medicine, in every form, is a failure and to restore freedom to the health-care market.[7]

Subsidizing a right to healthcare would encourage at least some to make less responsible choices. People would have little incentive to self-ration care for minor complaints; they would visit a dermatologist for a wart. Providers would also have incentive to offer unnecessary care, which would drive up costs for everyone.

A universal "right" to healthcare infringes on the rights of others.

Making healthcare a right for all means forcing the cooperation of many other people, primarily healthcare providers and taxpayers. Imposing duties on others, most often strangers, has the effect of violating *their* rights. As Thomas J. Bole III explains, "The difficulty is that rights to have one's need met or one's goods realized, positive rights, usually involve claims on the labors and resources of others. Positive rights circumscribe negative rights, the right to be left alone."[8]

It is important to note that although government can mandate universal healthcare insurance, government itself does not produce the care. People—doctors, nurses, technicians, and other skilled professionals—produce these services by means of their training, time, and skills. If universal healthcare is deemed a right, providers could be deprived of their rights to decide where to practice, which patients to see, and how many patients to accept. They might be forced to accept low fees set by the government and be told which treatments they must use. (Under the current system, providers may decide if they want to participate in Medicare and Medicaid and which private insurance they will accept.) If people can go to any healthcare provider and demand treatment, then caregivers and healthcare facilities might not be permitted to refuse anyone. If they did, people could file lawsuits claiming they did not get what they are entitled to. Scenarios like these violate a person's legal right to choose with whom they wish to contract. As Leonard Peikoff notes:

> There can be no such thing as a "right" to products or services created by the effort of others, and this most definitely includes medical products and services. . . .

You are free to see a doctor and pay him for his services—no one may forcibly prevent you from doing so. But you do not have a "right" to force the doctor to treat you without charge or to force others to pay for your treatment. The rights of some cannot require the coercion and sacrifice of others.[9]

Such a system can cause excellent caregivers to quit practicing and discourage others from entering the healthcare professions. This is already happening as doctors must work harder each year for less money. Additionally, citizens must rely on foreign-trained doctors—who may or may not have the same level of training as American doctors—to work in certain areas where recruiting physicians is difficult. Dr. Michael Hurd notes, "Health care is the consequence of heroic efforts on the part of individual doctors, who have every right to charge what the market permits. If we take away the right of medical professionals to

Arizona Proposition 101: The Freedom of Choice in Health Care Act

In November 2008, citizens in Arizona voted on an amendment to their state constitution that would protect the right to make individual healthcare choices without government interference. It was narrowly defeated by a vote of 50.2 percent to 49.8 percent. The following is an excerpt from the proposed amendment:

Because all people should have the right to make decisions about their health care, no law shall be passed that restricts a person's freedom of choice of private health care systems or private plans of any type. No law shall interfere with a person's or entity's right to pay directly for lawful medical services, nor shall any law impose a penalty or fine, of any type, for choosing to obtain or decline health care coverage or for participation in any particular health care system or plan.

set their own fees, we will undermine their independence and chase the best ones into early retirement."[10]

Programs to implement a right to universal healthcare would abridge the rights of many people in significant ways. It would compel taxpayers to fund services for others. People might be forced to buy health insurance even if they didn't want it. Healthy people might be compelled to buy more elaborate and costly coverage than they prefer. Employers of all sizes, including small businesses with limited resources, might be legally bound to cover all employees. This could force businesses to close, which would increase unemployment and in turn lower tax revenues for government programs. This kind of system also infringes on a consumer's right to trade freely with healthcare providers and reach a mutual agreement without government interference.

What do people owe to others who experience health problems? Illnesses and injuries arise primarily from individual circumstances, however unfortunate, and are usually not caused by outsiders or the larger society. Poor lifestyle choices may also play a role. People certainly may choose to help those in need, based on feelings of morality and compassion, but not because they owe them this assistance. The United States has a strong tradition of charity to those in need, based on voluntary giving, not a government mandate.

People disagree about what benefits should stem from a "right to healthcare."

Even if people were given a right to healthcare, how do we determine the scope of the benefits and how they should be delivered? Legal scholar and healthcare writer Richard A. Epstein observes, "No one believes that the right to health care is so absolute that it sweeps aside all claims to food, clothing, or shelter. Yet by the same token, the scope of a more circumscribed duty turns out, at a philosophical level, to be well-nigh indefinable, no matter how many times we intone the words 'reasonable,' 'decent,' 'basic,' 'adequate,' or 'necessary.'"[11]

Consider, for example, the World Health Organization's (WHO) definition of "health." Broad and ambiguous, it describes health as "a state of complete physical, mental, and social well-being and not merely the absence of disease or infirmity." Most people would agree that few, if any, human beings experience such a state of "complete" well-being in all of these areas throughout their lives.

Even if people agree on the idea of providing some healthcare for all, who will decide between needs and wants? This is especially challenging in today's world, where things people once viewed as a nuisance or a normal aspect of aging have been redefined as "illnesses" that can be fixed. These include infertility, impotence, and numerous other conditions, including "addictions" to behaviors like gambling and shopping. Some people might claim that their social and emotional well-being requires cosmetic surgery, hair transplants, or whiter teeth. Others might demand unusual forms of healthcare to suit their personal cultural or religious beliefs. Thomas Halper asks, "And why limit the entitlement to health care? Why not add food, clothing, shelter, Club Med, everything?"[12] Talking about rights and social obligations is meaningless unless people reach a consensus about what to deliver, and how.

Implementing a right to healthcare can lead to lower-quality care and rationing.

Developing entitlement programs based on the "right to health-care" entails difficult decisions and practical problems. People who talk of a right to healthcare seem to assume that the necessary resources are available to deliver that care and that the government is equipped to make healthcare decisions for all Americans. Another problem is that people would lose their private health plans and might not be entitled to the same services under a universal healthcare program. Further, a person who worked his or her way up to an executive position would be entitled to the same healthcare options as an unemployed person—a violation of the principle that people should receive due benefits from their talents and efforts.

The demand for healthcare will also likely exceed the capacity of the system. Universal access stemming from a right to healthcare would encourage a great deal of consumption, which may not match up with local resources. Other nations have realized that making healthcare a right means manipulating the delivery system in numerous ways and setting limits to make it affordable. The government might need to control fees for services and medical products. It would likely place limits on services, facilities, and technology and strictly limit access to expensive and scarce types of healthcare, meaning that people could wait weeks or even months for care. Writing about the "explicit rationing" that tends to occur in universal healthcare systems, authors Carolyn L. Engelhard and Arthur Garson Jr. note, "This type of moral framework is an awkward fit with the American preference for pluralism, individual freedoms, and limited government."[13]

In its role of guaranteeing healthcare, the government would, presumably, decide whose rights take precedence when multiple parties seek the same resources. Taken to its ultimate conclusion, this kind of system gives government the power to decide who lives or dies. Government agencies might decide questions like these: Do some illnesses deserve more attention than others? Is everyone equal in terms of healthcare rights, or do some people's needs take priority over others? Should a comatose elderly person receive kidney dialysis on par with a child who has a better chance of recovery? Should a convicted murderer receive the same care as a government official? Should medical technology costing millions of dollars be used to save extremely premature infants who will have severe long-term health problems? And how about "quality of life" issues? Will the right to healthcare include psychotherapy to deal with sexual dysfunction or gambling problems? Should the government move more resources to prevention and health education, which would leave even less money to provide actual care for the sick and injured?

Claiming a "right" to healthcare confuses the means with the ends.

If everyone has a "right" to healthcare, will that necessarily promote better health for all? Many people think not. As Thomas Halper explains, "It is not good health care that people desire, after all, but rather good health, and health care is only one of several means to that end."[14]

Research shows that more care does not always equal better health outcomes. In one study, people who used more services than others over a period of several years were not healthier at the end. RAND, a think tank, tracked 1,400 families over a period of three years and another 600 families for five years. All of them were examined thoroughly to check their health status before and after the study. RAND then tracked the use of services by people who had access to free care and those who had to pay a share of their insurance premiums and a copayment at the time of service. The people who had free care used 40 percent more services than those who had to pay, but, according to the authors of the study, "the 40 percent increase in services on the free-care plan had little or no measurable effect on health status for the average adult."[15]

Moving more public resources to healthcare can take attention and public funding away from other areas of life that also affect health and safety, such as education, public safety, environmental concerns, national security, and the overall problems resulting from poverty. Some states are already spending more of their budgets on healthcare than on education, yet education is a major factor in helping people to lift themselves out of poverty so they can buy things they need, including healthcare.

Moreover, there is a big difference between universal access to healthcare and healthcare itself. People who have government insurance still might not receive care if resources are unavailable in their area or caregivers cannot afford to see them for the fees government sets. This is an issue with both Medicare and especially Medicaid, because these programs pay doctors and hospitals lower fees than private insurance. Under our current system, physicians who work in places where it is difficult to recruit doctors, such as rural Mississippi, actually earn more than their counterparts in urban areas. Would this be the case with universal healthcare?

Trade-offs are bound to occur, and they can diminish the quality of care. Thomas Halper points out that achieving "the greater good for the greater number" often comes at a price, and that excellence and equality are rarely achieved simultaneously.[16] He notes, for example, that achieving excellence can require concentrating resources at a major teaching hospital, while achieving equality would require moving those resources to places where people need doctors.

Summary
The idea of a "right to healthcare" sounds admirable, but this kind of thinking leads to open-ended, expensive entitlements. Numerous problems arise as people wrestle with the scope of such a right and try to implement it in a world of finite resources and huge demand. Even if people agree that healthcare for all is good, it does not necessarily follow that everyone has a "right" to healthcare, especially since these services must be provided by others, whose rights must be taken into account in the process. There is no inherent right to receive goods or services from other people who may or may not choose to give them. This approach gives government too much power over people's lives and can lead to rationing and a lower quality of care. The problems in the healthcare system require a different approach, with less government involvement, not more. As Michael Burton asks, "What problem could not be solved, simply by inventing a new right?"[17]

The United States Should Adopt a National Single-Payer Healthcare System

In the late 1980s, Taiwan decided to change its healthcare system. A capitalist democracy in Asia, Taiwan was then using a private insurance model, but about 57 percent of its citizens lacked insurance. Hongyen Chang was part of the commission responsible for planning a more modern and effective system. During an interview in 2008, he said that his government studied healthcare systems around the world and evaluated them in light of this old Chinese proverb: "The track of the previous cart is the teacher of the following cart." Said Chang, "If they were trapped in trouble, avoid that track. Find a new track."[1]

Taiwan chose a single-payer system, which took effect in 1995. The results? By 2007, 97 percent of all Taiwanese had health coverage through the government plan. Healthcare administrative costs were 2 percent, the lowest in the world, and Taiwan was spending 6.23 percent of its gross domestic product (GDP) on healthcare, compared to 16 percent in the United

States.[2] Surveys also showed a high level of satisfaction with the new system, which offered modern care from well-trained professionals.[3]

Other countries have used single-payer systems to achieve universal access to healthcare. What is a single-payer system? This means that payments for healthcare come from one source, the government, which negotiates with providers to set fees. Americans who support such a plan often point to the Canadian system, since Canada resembles the United States in terms of geography, economics, culture, and a decentralized style of government. In Canada, public financing pays for services delivered by private doctors and hospitals. Canadians receive a health security card that verifies their insurance, while people in Taiwan use a "smart card."

Private healthcare insurance, or public? This is a major ongoing healthcare debate. In the United States, private insurance has maintained its edge, and special-interest groups have fought against programs that would reduce their role in healthcare. Support has been building for a single-payer system, however. In a poll conducted in December 2007, 65 percent of the respondents said the United States "should adopt a universal health insurance program in which everyone is covered under a program like Medicare that is run by the government and financed by taxpayers."[4]

Opponents have called single-payer insurance plans "socialized medicine." In a socialized system, however, the government also owns and operates services. The United States does, in fact, have a form of socialized medical care. The Veterans Health Administration (VHA), a government body, owns and runs healthcare facilities for veterans. Although the VHA rations care to veterans according to a number of priority factors, the administration has received awards for excellence and efficiency in healthcare delivery. The United States also operates a single-payer program in the form of Medicare, which provides benefits to the elderly.

Single-payer plans provide universal and equitable coverage. They are simpler to administer and thus more efficient and cost-effective than the current fragmented, profit-driven U.S. system. This benefits both consumers and healthcare providers. Citizens receive uniform comprehensive benefits, including preventive care and ongoing care for chronic conditions, which can prevent higher costs later on. Covering all Americans would give everyone a stake in the quality of the system and create the largest pool for spreading risks and sharing costs. With a one-tiered system, people can access the same level of care based on medical need, not economic assets. Each year, an estimated 18,000 Americans die because they lack health insurance.[5] "You can't discriminate based on the size of your wallet on something as important as health care," says Michael McBane, coordinator of the Canadian Health Coalition, an advocacy group.[6]

A single-payer system covers everyone from birth to death with portable and equitable insurance.
Single-payer plans are not tied to age, employment, income level, place of residence, or health status. When insurance stays with the person, people need not fear losing their coverage if they lose their job or change jobs, become self-employed, are divorced, or retire before age 65. Employers would not choose people's health plans, so employees would not have to change plans or pay higher fees if an employer decided to pay less.

Such a plan would solve the widespread problems of noncoverage and underinsurance. People who become ill or have preexisting conditions need not go without insurance or pay steep premiums. Insurance companies could no longer "skim the risk pool" and deny people coverage for various reasons. Each year, thousands of people are dropped by their insurers because they become ill or failed to mention minor health problems when they applied for insurance—a practice known as rescission.[7] A single-payer national health plan would prevent such problems.

Single-payer systems reduce administrative costs, and that money can be shifted to healthcare.

Single-payer plans save money by reducing overhead (which includes profits), and by simplifying billing and payment procedures. Studies by the U.S. General Accounting Office (GAO), Congressional Budget Office, and others show that these costs add up to many billions of dollars each year. In the United States, administrative costs now run 50 percent to 100 percent higher than the costs in nations that use single-payer systems.[8] Comparing costs in Canada and the United States, two economists note, "Before the full implementation of the Canadian system in 1971, the funding system and the health costs as a share of gross national product (GNP) were virtually identical in both countries at about 7 percent of GNP."[9] Since then, the U.S. figure has risen much faster than Canada's. In 2004, the *New England Journal of Medicine* reported that the United States could save $286 billion by shifting to single-payer insurance and that this money was enough to provide healthcare to everyone who was uninsured.[10] In 2008, Physicians for a National Health Plan (PNHP) estimated the savings at $350 billion.[11]

Current methods of paying for healthcare in the United States are complicated and time-consuming. Healthcare providers deal

---

QUOTABLE

Uwe Reinhardt, Ph.D.

There is no other country in the OECD [Organization for Economic Cooperation and Development] where any citizen has ever been jailed for failure to pay a hospital bill, only in America. And I would ask my fellow citizens: Are you comfortable with that?

Source: PBS, Frontline: "Sick Around the World." April 15, 2008. http://www.pbs.org/wgbh/pages/frontline/sickaroundtheworld/interviews/reinhardt.html.

At what cost?

When adjusted for inflation, U.S. physicians' net incomes have declined since 1995, while insurers' administrative costs have risen.

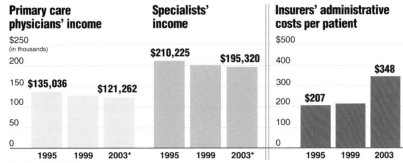

Primary care physicians' income

$250 (in thousands)
200
150 $135,036
100 $121,262
50
0
    1995   1999   2003*

Specialists' income

$210,225 $195,320

    1995   1999   2003*

Insurers' administrative costs per patient

$500
400        $348
300
200 $207
100
0
    1995   1999   2003

*Latest statistics available

Source: Center for Studying Health System Change, Centers for Medicare and Medicaid Services, Office of the Actuary, National Health Statistics Group
Graphic: Laurie Joseph, Dallas Morning News

© 2008 MCT

Above, charts show the decline in U.S. physicians' incomes against the increase in insurers' administrative costs. The years 1995, 1999, and 2003 are compared.

with hundreds of different insurance plans from commercial carriers and self-insured businesses. They also bill federal agencies, including the Centers for Medicare and Medicaid Services. States, counties, and municipalities pay bills for certain hospitals and Medicaid patients, and patients themselves pay some or all of their expenses. Healthcare providers must follow the various third-party requirements for authorizing services and processing claims.

This means higher administrative costs for providers, who must pay staff to handle billing and other insurance issues, including obtaining advance authorizations for tests and treatments. Those costs translate into higher fees. Dr. John A. Glaspy, a physician in Los Angeles, said, "We have one employee just getting radiological approvals, eight to 10 a day. That's $45,000 in salary, plus benefits, not going to health care. It can take us a whole day just to find out who to get the authorization from."[12] The percentage of U.S. healthcare workers in administration (not including health insurance administrators) grew from 18.2 percent to 27.3 between 1969 and 1999. In Canada, these figures went from 16 percent to 19.1 percent between 1971 and 1996. This single factor added an average $752 more to healthcare costs for each American.[13]

In other developed nations, one or a few organizations pay hospitals and physicians, and these nations have simpler and more standardized procedures for setting fees. In Canada, the provider enters the patient's health card into the system and then marks the type of service that was performed, using a form or a computer disc. Taiwan uses cost-saving information technology (IT) that is considered state-of-the-art.

Using private insurance companies as third-party payers increases healthcare costs in other ways. Authors Barlett and Steele note, "In truth, it is the private market that has created a massive bureaucracy, one that dwarfs the size and costs of Medicare, the most efficiently run health insurance program in America in terms of administrative costs."[14] A survey of insurance and medical executives in 2007 showed that more than 30 cents of every healthcare dollar was going to overhead, for a total of about $630 billion.[15] This overhead includes processing claims, advertising and marketing, building and furnishing business facilities, executive and staff salaries, bonuses, and profits. The companies pay employees to negotiate fees with healthcare providers, determine which providers should be paid and how much, review people's eligibility for coverage, dispute claims, and pay claims. The CEOs of large health insurance companies often earn millions in salary and other benefits each year. In 2005, *Forbes* magazine reported the total compensation given to the CEOs of two of the nation's largest health insurance companies: William W. McGuire, CEO of United Healthgroup, received $124.8 million,[16] while John W. Rowe, the CEO of Aetna Inc., received $22.2 million.[17] Insurance-industry profits reached $57.5 billion in 2006.[18] In the Medicaid insurance system, states spend time and money determining who is eligible for services, because people come in and out of the system, based on their income level. A single-payer plan makes many of these administrative tasks unnecessary, and profits are not involved.

Critics of universal healthcare often ask: Where would the nation get the money to cover everyone? Experts have said the United States could cover all medically indicated care for every citizen without additional expenditures, because administrative costs and current insurance premiums could be shifted to care instead.[19] In 2005, Paul Krugman, winner of the 2008 Nobel Memorial Prize in Economic Sciences, called the single-payer system "good economics" and wrote, "The great advantage of universal, government-provided health insurance is lower costs. . . . Medicare has much lower administrative costs than private insurance." Krugman pointed out that the savings from a single-payer system would be "far more than the cost of covering all those now insured."[20] The government of Colorado hired the Lewin Group Technical Assessment to analyze how well four different health-plan proposals might work for the state. In its 2007 report, the Lewin Group said that a single-payer plan was the only one that would achieve universal coverage and also save money—about $1.4 billion a year.[21] Numerous other state and federal studies have reached similar conclusions.

Other countries have reduced costs by replacing private profit-making insurance companies with one-payment system. During the first year of its national health-insurance program, Taiwan covered 41 percent more people yet costs only rose from 4.8 percent to 5.39 percent the next year. Before the plan was implemented, costs were rising about 13 percent each year. Since then, the increase has ranged between 3 percent to 6 percent.[22]

Single-payer systems offer secure payments and more autonomy for providers.

In addition to simpler billing procedures, single-payer plans offer other economic advantages to physicians, hospitals, and other providers, who would not have to deliver free care to the uninsured or wonder if bills will be paid. Insurance companies may delay and/or deny payments, and in some cases, hospitals accumulate millions of dollars in unpaid bills.[23] Physicians spend valuable resources trying to collect payments and disputed insurance claims. Statistics show that physicians, hospitals, and other providers are more likely to receive payments from Medicare than from private insurance companies.[24] Physicians could maintain doctor-patient relations longer, for better continuity of care, when patients are not forced to change doctors because they have changed insurance policies that use a different "network" of providers.

For these and other reasons, an increasing number of American physicians now support a single-payer system. They include Physicians for a National Health Plan, Society for General Internal Medicine, and the American College of Physicians.[25] A 2008 survey taken among U.S. physicians showed that 59 percent favored national health insurance; only 32 percent opposed it. In 2002, those numbers were 49 percent and 40 percent, respectively. Dr. Ronald Ackerman, who worked on the study, said, "Across the board, more physicians feel that our fragmented and for-profit insurance system is obstructing good patient care and a majority now support national insurance as the remedy."[26]

Single-payer insurance would benefit the U.S. economy.

A single-payer plan that covers everyone would boost the U.S. economy, both nationally and on the local level. Civil servants would be covered along with other citizens, so states and municipalities would no longer bear these costs.

American businesses do not have a level playing field as they compete with businesses in countries that have universal health insurance. In 2006, for example, health benefits for U.S. auto-workers added $1,500 to the cost of a medium-sized car, while the cost in Japan was about $500.[27] As health insurance costs rise at rates of 14 to 18 percent annually, many U.S. companies cannot afford it, while they spend additional money paying employees to handle health insurance matters.

With this burden removed, companies would not have to cut personnel or forgo improvements to pay health benefits for employees and their families and, in some cases, retirees. They could invest more in their businesses and even hire more people, including older employees and others who would have cost more to insure. Companies might even be able to increase wages and strengthen their pension funds. A single-payer program could also improve relations between management and labor by preventing conflicts and strikes over health benefits. Freed from the burden of insuring employees, more people might also start new businesses.

Along with these improvements, the economy could realize the benefits of having a healthier workforce that does not fear the cost of illness. People can remain in their jobs out of choice, not because they dread losing employer-based insurance if they return to school, change jobs, or start their own business.

Society also benefits when people do not go bankrupt or lose their homes because of expensive health problems. In recent years, studies showed that medical causes were associated with more than half of all home foreclosures in the United States.[28] In 2008, these foreclosures were affecting 1 in every 54 families.[29] Real estate values sink when too many homes are on the market, and that helps to drag down the overall econcomy.

Fears of rationing are exaggerated, and rationing already occurs in the U.S. system.

One of the main objections to single-payer insurance is the idea that health services will be rationed. Critics say that people in

Great Britain and Canada, for example, lack access to the latest treatments and must wait to see doctors, especially specialists. Concern over waiting lists in Canada grew during the 1990s when the system experienced funding problems. The Canadian system is financed through federal and provincial contributions, and the federal government reduced its share between 1980 and 2001. Analysts say funding was inadequate to deliver services.

In 2005, the Canadian Supreme Court ruled, by a margin of one vote, that the ban on private insurance violated citizens' rights under the Quebec Charter of Human Rights because waiting times for some services were too long. The court did not find that the ban on private health insurance violated section 7 (the right to life, liberty, and security of the person) of the Canadian Charter of Rights and Freedoms. Canada's federal health minister, Ujjal Dosanjh, said, "We have to strengthen the public health care system so there is no need for a private system, and we are on the way to doing that."[30] In Quebec, where the lawsuit originated, officials took action to improve the delivery system. In February 2006, the governor of Quebec announced that government would set guaranteed waiting times for certain procedures, including cardiac surgery, cataract removals, knee and hip replacements, and some radiation treatments. That year, Statistics Canada showed that 80 percent of Canadians were satisfied with their access to healthcare.[31] Waiting times to see doctors declined between 2007 and 2008, although they remained lengthy. The wait time between a referral from a general practitioner to consult with a specialist declined from an average of 9.2 weeks to 8.5 weeks and the wait time between seeing a specialist and receiving treatment went from 9.1 weeks to 8.7 weeks.[32]

Critics say that many Canadian physicians relocate to the United States so they can earn more money and practice in a private system. Though some physicians have left, 2004 saw an increase in the number of Canadian-trained physicians who returned to Canada.[33] The Canadian government has expanded medical school residency programs to increase the number of physicians.

Supporters of Canada's single-payer plan remain committed to a one-tiered system that discourages privatization and for-profit healthcare. They believe that the regulations banning physicians from practicing private medicine if they receive government payment are necessary to prevent longer waits for public services. Deborah Tamlyn, president of the Canadian Nurses Association, notes:

> Canadians do not want to become a society where only the wealthy can afford hip replacements. We must find innovative solutions to deliver care if we are going to sustain and revitalize our publicly funded, not-for-profit and publicly administered health system ... Promoting privately owned health services will lead to a deterioration of public health service delivery in Canada.[34]

Canada is also finding ways to improve efficiency, including the use of research to determine the most effective treatments. Dr. Colleen M. Flood, the scientific director of the Canadian Institutes of Health Research, wrote, "Canada's health-care system needs reform—but reform based on the best available evidence and guided by Canadian values. CIHR-IHSPR [Institute of Health Services and Policy Research] is committed to providing evidence-based solutions that will improve the health-care system."[35]

Would rationing and long waiting lists occur in the United States? Single-payer advocates say no, because, unlike Canada, the nation has abundant healthcare resources already in place. Dr. Ronald Glasser points out:

> An axiom of economics holds that nothing can be rationed that is itself not scarce, and, absent evidence of infinite demand and infinite cost, you can't ration

health care when there are more than enough doctors, hospitals, and high-tech equipment distributed throughout the country to do everything and anything that needs to be done. American health care is an unsaturated demand market, and in such markets "rationing" is simply a code word for not spending the money to take care of the poor, the uninsured, the underinsured, and the high-risk patient.[36]

Besides, the United States already rations care but in a different way, based on the ability to pay and type of insurance. People without money are "rationed out" of earlier care that might prevent or control disease. They are more likely to seek costlier later-stage care in hospitals and emergency rooms (ERs). Some ERs have been flooded with patients seeking free routine care, which causes longer waiting times and other problems. A study conducted from 1997 to 2004 found that the median waiting time to see a physician in the ER jumped from 22 minutes to 30 minutes.[37] Researchers say these longer waits result from increased visits to the ER and the closing of many ERs, both of which spring from the problem of uninsured patients.

Other kinds of rationing occur when insurance company plans block people from visiting specialists without permission,

QUOTABLE

Robert H. LeBow, M.D.

The definition of U.S.–style rationing is: (a) If you can afford it, you get it. (b) If you can't afford it, you either can't or won't get it unless (c) it's a dire emergency and (d) you're lucky enough to catch the problem in time and survive.

Source: Robert H. LeBow, M.D., *Health Care Meltdown: Confronting the Myths and Fixing Our Failing System*. Chambersburg, Pa.: A. C. Hood, 2003, p. 29.

make people wait for approval, or deny treatments to cut costs. Dr. Linda Peeno, a former medical reviewer for large health insurance companies who now focuses on medical ethics, discussed these matters when she testified before Congress in 1996. In a 2002 interview with the *Washington Post,* Peeno said:

> The idea behind rationing (if we really even need to do that) is that if we deny something to one person, we give the savings to someone else who benefits more. That is a societal decision, not a business decision. We are the only country that rations health care by the persons who benefit economically from those decisions.[38]

With a single-payer program, the determination of benefits is more visible to the public, and government can make decisions based on careful consideration of people's needs for preventive services, continuity of care, and medically necessary treatment. Says Dr. Linda Peeno, "I am not convinced we need to ration care. But if we do, then we have to have an ethical system that makes fair decisions, and ensures that the money saved goes back into the health system to benefit patients, not stockholders."[39] Dr. Susan Rosenthal concludes, "The only way to ensure that everyone has access is to make medical care a social priority and fully fund it. That means no rationing of *any kind.*"[40]

A single-payer public program can focus on people and quality standards, not profits.

Critics say government should not have the power to set healthcare policies and administer the system, but are consumers better served by a profit-based system? Health insurance companies may base decisions about coverage, restrictions, and payments on what will make the company prosper. The goals of private insurance companies do not necessarily foster better healthcare and may even conflict with that goal. In the area of prevention, private insurance companies have less incentive to encourage

On the critical list

Lacking universal health care insurance, Americans get the poorest care and spend the most for it, compared to five other nations studied.

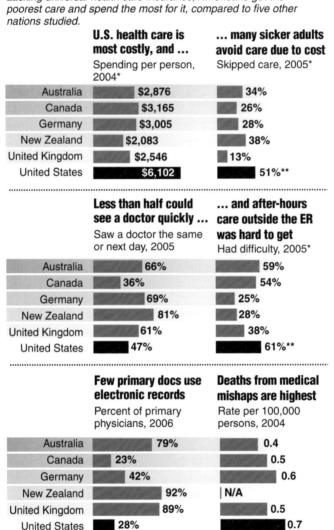

U.S. health care is most costly, and ...
Spending per person, 2004*

Australia	$2,876
Canada	$3,165
Germany	$3,005
New Zealand	$2,083
United Kingdom	$2,546
United States	$6,102

... many sicker adults avoid care due to cost
Skipped care, 2005*

Australia	34%
Canada	26%
Germany	28%
New Zealand	38%
United Kingdom	13%
United States	51%**

Less than half could see a doctor quickly ...
Saw a doctor the same or next day, 2005

Australia	66%
Canada	36%
Germany	69%
New Zealand	81%
United Kingdom	61%
United States	47%

... and after-hours care outside the ER was hard to get
Had difficulty, 2005*

Australia	59%
Canada	54%
Germany	25%
New Zealand	28%
United Kingdom	38%
United States	61%**

Few primary docs use electronic records
Percent of primary physicians, 2006

Australia	79%
Canada	23%
Germany	42%
New Zealand	92%
United Kingdom	89%
United States	28%

Deaths from medical mishaps are highest
Rate per 100,000 persons, 2004

Australia	0.4
Canada	0.5
Germany	0.6
New Zealand	N/A
United Kingdom	0.5
United States	0.7

*Adjusted for differences in cost of living
**57 percent of low-income adults skip care, 70 percent have difficulty after hours
Source: Commonwealth Fund International Health Policy Survey
Graphic: Pat Carr, Melina Yingling
© 2007 MCT

Here, charts compare the U.S. healthcare system to the universal healthcare systems of five other nations: Australia, Canada, Germany, New Zealand, and the United Kingdom.

preventive care than a single-payer plan that must cover people from birth through death. Physicians for a National Health Plan notes that "while prevention improves health and may cut costs ten years down the line, insurers operate on a much shorter time-frame."[41]

Common sense can prevail in a public and transparent system in which everyone has a stake in good health outcomes. A nonprofit program designed for the public interest can more effectively promote health and allocate resources with policies that focus on the two vital parties in a healthcare transaction: patients and providers. The government program can set standards of care based on research, not profits, in its role of assuring adequate and appropriate care. It will have immense bargaining power to negotiate with companies that sell drugs and medical equipment. In Canada, for example, prescription drug prices are controlled and more affordable, which has led some Americans to buy medications from Canada. With a single point of accountability, Americans can voice their concerns to elected officials who are accountable to the public.

Critics also say people have less "choice" with a single insurance plan. Yet, "choice" in insurance plans has created a situation in which people are unclear about the various provisions in the plans and do not fully understand their coverage. Insurance plans, in turn, limit choices and treatment options. In April 2002, health policy expert Rima Cohen told Congress to beware of "calls for more choice." She pointed out, "I think all Americans want choice of their health care providers. I don't see individuals clamoring as much for their choice of health plans, their ... choice of benefit packages."[42] Single-payer plans let people choose their physicians and hospitals.

In the United States, Medicare shows that a single-payer plan works, and Medicare patients express higher levels of satisfaction with their coverage and access to care than people with private insurance. They were more likely to rate their insurance as "excellent" and less likely to report negative experiences with their plan.[43]

As for Canada's single-payer system, despite the critics, its true measure can be found in health outcomes. A team of Canadian and U.S. researchers set out to answer this question: "Are there differences in death and disease rates in patients suffering from similar medical conditions treated in Canada versus those treated in the United States?" After analyzing data from 1955 to 2003, they found that in 14 studies, Canadians had better health outcomes, as opposed to five that favored the United States. In the other 19 studies, they found equivalent or mixed results. One researcher, Dr. P. J. Devereux, a Canadian physician, noted that the United States spent more than twice as much per person than Canada did. He said the study showed "that despite an enormous investment in money, we do not see better outcomes" in the United States.[44]

Summary

All things considered, a single-payer system is the most logical way to insure all Americans while keeping costs at a reasonable level. The annual savings, involving hundreds of billions of dollars in overhead, can go where it belongs—to patients and caregivers, not profits and administrative costs. Patients will no longer need to fear the lack of insurance or endure additional pain and suffering because they cannot afford healthcare or medications. This kind of universal plan recognizes the dignity of every human being and promotes equity, as well as better public health. Noting the success of single-payer systems, Physicians for a National Health Program remarks, "We do not need to reinvent the wheel to reform health care. But we do need to defeat an insurance industry that would deny us the rational solution that would finally bring health security and safety to the people of this country."[45]

The United States Should Not Adopt a National Single-Payer Healthcare System

The Canadian single-payer system is often cited as the model the United States should follow. Though people have called the Canadian approach equitable and altruistic, it suffers from long waits for service, personnel shortages, inadequate long-term care facilities for the elderly, crowded emergency rooms, shortages of high-tech devices, and lack of innovation. The annual costs in Canada also exceed costs in some Organization for Economic Cooperation and Development nations that have demonstrated better health outcomes.

Changing to a single-payer system would remove the choices Americans now have through the competitive insurance markets. Government bureaucracy would likely produce more inefficiency and create rationing and longer waits for care. Poor working conditions, including low fees, would lead to shortages of healthcare professionals. A single-payer system would not necessarily reduce costs and might even increase them because more access to free or inexpensive services can lead to overuse. As Susan Pisano, vice president of the American Association of Health Plans, noted in 2002, a single-payer plan "would lead to the creation of a large federal bureaucracy that would be less responsive and actually raise issues of cost, access, and quality more than it would solve them."[1]

Single-payer systems create ineffective and unjust government monopolies.

With a single-payer system, a healthcare monopoly would result, with just one buyer involved in the healthcare market.

FROM THE BENCH

Supreme Court of Canada, *Chaoulli v. Quebec* [2005] 1 S.C.R. 791

In 2005, the Canadian Supreme Court heard the case of *Chaoulli v. Quebec (Attorney General)*. In keeping with the Canada Health Act of 1971, Quebec and other provinces banned the purchase of private health insurance and forbade physicians who treat private patients from accepting fees from the public insurance program. Dr. Jacques Chaoulli, a physician, and his patient George Zeliotis filed a lawsuit challenging the government's ban on private insurance after Zeliotis was kept waiting a year for hip replacement surgery. In its 4-to-3 ruling, the high court struck down the Quebec law:

> The evidence in this case shows that delays in the public health care system are widespread, and that, in some serious cases, patients die as a result of waiting lists for public health care. The evidence also demonstrates that the prohibition against private health insurance and its consequence of denying people vital health care result in physical and psychological suffering that meets a threshold test of seriousness.

The court also noted: "[W]aiting lists for health care services have resulted in deaths, have increased the length of time that patients have to be in pain and have impaired patients' ability to enjoy any real quality of life."

The government would have the power to decide who receives what care and when, as well as to set the terms and prices for healthcare providers. Decisions in a government system tend to become politicized, and that would occur with healthcare as well. Healthcare expert Michael Bliss describes the pitfalls in this kind of system when he writes: "[R]emove an industry from market conditions, replace price signaling with administrative fiat, outlaw competition, and you create the classic conditions for inefficiency, declining productivity, and gradually increasing consumer dissatisfaction."[2]

In Canada, government regulations ban physicians who see private patients from taking part in the public-funded system. Public funds are not used to pay the private sector, and physicians cannot extra-bill public patients. As a result, physicians and other providers are pressured to practice only publicly funded medicine in which the government sets all the rules and fee schedules. At times, Canadian healthcare personnel have been forced to strike for better pay and working conditions. In 1998, physicians and nurses in different parts of Canada went on strike to protest being overworked and underpaid.[3] Between 1997 and 2002, three strikes occurred among healthcare workers in Saskatchewan. In 2002, a union made up of 2,500 workers, including hospital pharmacists, public health inspectors, and social workers, sought higher wages and better working conditions.[4]

As the Canadian Supreme Court said in 2005, the government system created "a virtual monopoly" where delays in treatment can adversely affect health. That monopoly, said the court, failed "to provide public health care of a reasonable standard within a reasonable time."[5] The government forced people to take part in a single publicly funded program that supposedly gave them access to healthcare but did not provide readily available services, and people could not buy private insurance to finance private care. For these reasons, other Canadians have also filed lawsuits protesting the government's monopoly on healthcare insurance.

Supporters of Canada's system say that rules are needed to protect the country's publicly funded healthcare. Other nations in the OECD, however, have achieved better results by letting citizens use private healthcare even as they fund national health insurance. In its decision in *Chaoulli v. Quebec*, the court cited evidence showing that Switzerland, Germany, France, and other countries manage to deliver "medical services that are superior to and more affordable than the services that are presently available in Canada."[6] Switzerland chose not to implement a single-payer system. The country's president, Pascal Couchepin, explained:

> We rejected it because we think if you have a single payer, which is also the only [party] who makes contracts with . . . all the providers, it will be dangerous, because there is too much power in the hands of the health insurance system. We think that if there is competition between the health insurance companies, there will be a certain control among themselves; they will denounce the excesses of the others . . . they will try to provide better services, and so you can compare.[7]

A single-payer monopoly limits people's fundamental rights and choices. In a free society, people should not be forced into one national program with only one tier of health insurance coverage. While increasing government control over healthcare, a one-tiered single-payer system minimizes individual rights. It forces healthy people to pay—through taxes, premiums, or both—for coverage they do not necessarily want or need. People in good health might well prefer to purchase less expensive coverage with limited benefits, not more costly coverage with benefits they might never use. With a single-payer system where everyone has the same benefit package, they have no choice.

People's rights are abridged in other ways as well, if they are denied the freedom to use their legally earned resources to buy healthcare outside the system. People with more means should be free to obtain things they want and need—including more comprehensive or additional healthcare coverage.

A lack of competition has serious consequences. Authors Nadeem Esmail and Michael Walker write:

> Without effective choice, health care delivery becomes a common, uncontested standard, leaving patients in a situation where they cannot protest for better quality by choosing to purchase health services from a different provider. Monopoly provision of care also abolishes the need for hospitals to be efficient and innovative due to lack of competition.[8]

A competitive private sector, these analysts claim, "can also serve as a measure of quality and availability of health services in the public sector, as well as competition with the public sector for patient care."[9]

Rationing and long waits for services are common in Canada's single-payer system.

People in a single-payer system can encounter problems with access, including long waits for appointments and services, especially sophisticated treatments and new technology. Because the government sets an annual cap on healthcare expenditures, the scope of health services must then fit within that budget. A report issued by the Fraser Institute in 2008 says that the health-care system in Canada is "burdened with lengthy wait lists and aging medical technology."[10] The idea of universal, free health-care means little if people cannot receive the care and services they need in a timely fashion.

Supporters of Canada's single-payer system note that Canada spends less each year on healthcare than the United States, in terms of the cost per person and the amount of GDP. To hold down costs, government limits the number of doctors, specialists, high-tech equipment, diagnostic tests, operating room hours, medications, and expensive treatments. These services are not as widely available as they are in the United States, so people must line up to receive them. Supporters of the single-payer system also say the U.S. system is more robust than the Canadian system, and therefore waits would not be as bad. Yet this argument ignores the crucial role that the free market has played in creating the U.S. healthcare system. A single-payer system, in which people and companies are not rewarded for their quality work, could likely diminish the number of people interested in medical careers or the number of companies interested in medical innovations.

For relatively healthy people, such a system might be adequate, since it offers Canadians free primary care, including physicals with a general practitioner, vision screenings, immunizations, and other basics. People who become seriously ill, however, wait for appointments with specialists, diagnostic tests, and treatments longer, on average, than people in the United States. After first waiting for their consultation with a specialist, they may wait weeks and even months for a biopsy, MRI, radiation treatments, or heart bypass or other surgery. During these waits, their health can deteriorate further. The results of one study released in 2008 showed that mortality rates for people with breast and prostate cancer are higher in Canada than they are in the United States. The results of the first five-continent study of cancer survival rates show that Americans had higher five-year survival rates for breast and prostate cancers than Canadians. For all five types of cancers studied, survival rates in the United States were 91.9 percent versus 82.5 percent in Canada and an even lower rate of 57.1 percent across Europe. This study looked at more than 2 million cancer patients in 31 countries.[11]

Although the government said it would address waiting lists after the court's ruling in *Chaoulli v. Quebec,* the median waiting time for patients between referral and surgery or other treatment reached a new high of 18.3 weeks in 2007, according to an annual report from the Fraser Institute. Waiting times increased 97 percent over a 14-year period.[12] The waiting time between referral by the general practitioner and consultation with a specialist also increased, from 8.8 weeks in 2006 to 9.2 weeks in 2007. Some of the longest waits involved orthopedic surgery (38.1 weeks) and neurosurgery (27.2 weeks). Waits for diagnostic tests were likewise long. Across the country, the median wait for a CT scan was 4.8 weeks, with a median wait of 10.1 weeks for an MRI.[13]

Problems persisted in 2008, when people in Saskatchewan were waiting an average of 28.8 weeks from the time they saw their general practitioner to the time they received specialized treatment. In Nova Scotia, the average total wait time was 27.6 weeks. These waiting times increased between 2007 and 2008.[14]

Does increased funding solve this problem? In its annual reports on waiting times for health services in Canada, the Fraser Institute noted that investing millions of dollars in the last decade had not produced significant improvements. In 2007, Tasha Kheiriddin, the Quebec director of the Fraser Institute, noted, "What this tells us is spending more money in the system does not decrease wait times. In fact, it's the opposite result, so we have to look at other solutions."[15]

QUOTABLE

Nadeem Esmail, Director of Health System Performance Studies, Fraser Institute

It's becoming clearer that Canada's current health-care system cannot meet the needs of Canadians in a timely and efficient manner, unless you consider access to a waiting list timely and efficient.

Source: Nadeem Esmail, "Waiting Your Turn: Hospital Waiting Lists in Canada." Fraser Institute, 2007.

Single-payer systems cause problems for healthcare providers, and adverse working conditions can lead to personnel shortages.
Shortages of medical personnel have been a problem in Canada, and this reflects poor working conditions. One report concluded that "system support has not kept pace with public support" for the national health program. In this report, general practitioners noted that they were increasingly forced to care for more patients, including more elderly patients and more seriously ill patients, due to the long wait times for specialized care. These burdens reduced their ability to provide continuing and preventive care and led fewer medical students to choose general practice as a career.[16] In a national survey of more than 20,000 Canadian physicians and doctors-in-training, 75 percent said that inadequate funding, a shortage of physicians and other health professionals, and paperwork and bureaucracy limited the amount and kind of care they wanted to deliver.[17] Family physicians expressed the most concern.

As a result, people in Canada have experienced problems finding a general practitioner. The Canadian Medical Association estimated that about 12 percent of the population did not have a family doctor in 2004.[18] The situation was still serious in 2008, when an estimated 4 to 5 million Canadians did not have a family doctor. CMA president Brian Day said that to meet the minimum standards set by the OECD, Canada would need to add 26,000 doctors at once.[19] The problem is expected to worsen because the population of doctors is aging, with an average age of 50 in 2008. In a report from the Heritage Foundation, author Kevin C. Fleming notes, "As of 2005, 43 percent of Ontario's 929 anesthesiologists were over the age of 50, and in addition to a regular 50-hour workweek, 40 percent of anesthesiologists worked every fourth night in hospital providing emergency coverage."[20]

A number of physicians who trained in Canada have left to practice in the United States and elsewhere. A study released in 2007 showed that during the past 30 years, about 19,000 physicians who trained in Canada relocated to the United States. About 8,162 Canadian-trained physicians were practicing in the United States in 2006, which amounts to one in nine Canadian-trained physicians. Author James Arvantes points out, "That figure ... is equivalent to having two average-sized Canadian medical schools dedicated entirely to producing physicians for the United States."[21]

In 2003, journalist Clifford Krauss interviewed two neurosurgeons who planned to relocate from Windsor, Canada, to nearby Detroit, Michigan. Between 1996 and 2002, 49 neurosurgeons left Canada, leaving just 241 neurosurgeons to serve the entire nation. The neurosurgeons in Windsor told Krauss their hospitals did not have enough anesthesiologists and nurses or adequate equipment. Dr. Siva Sriharan said, "It's not about the money. We can't do our job properly with operating time so extremely limited here."[22]

Reductions in medical staff mean that more people go outside the country, often to the United States, for deliveries, tests, surgery, and other healthcare. The Fraser Institute found that an estimated 33,492 Canadians went outside of Canada for nonemergency treatment in 2008.[23] Dr. Bernard Golnik treated Canadian women who needed prenatal care they could not receive at home. In an interview, he said, "In order to serve the masses they have been forced to place limits on technology. That's not something I'd be comfortable with."[24]

After the 2005 Supreme Court ruling in *Chaoulli,* Dr. Albert Schumacher, president of the Canadian Medical Association, noted that his patients had gone to nearby Detroit for their computed tomography (CT) because of the long wait in Canada. He said, "There are tens of thousands of Mr. Zeliotis out there languishing on waiting lists."[25]

Cost and benefit comparisons between the U.S. and Canadian systems may be misleading.

People who compare costs and benefits of healthcare systems in the United States and Canada overlook several key points. For instance, more elderly people receive healthcare in the United States, and Canada's costs would rise if it had the same percentage of elderly. The U.S. healthcare system delivers care to many more war veterans, victims of violence, teen mothers (who are more likely to have low birth-weight babies), substance abusers, and people with smoking-related diseases. Physicians and other caregivers pay more for professional liability insurance in the United States because of the higher incidence of malpractice cases. The United States puts far more money into medical research and development, and some analysts say these funds could be regarded as investments rather than "costs."

Moreover, thousands of Canadians pay for healthcare in the United States and other countries each year. These costs are not added to Canada's budget, yet they represent healthcare expenditures for Canadians. Health benefits also occur when people with serious conditions obtain timelier treatment in the United States. For example, in 2006, Lindsay McCreith of Newmarket, Canada, suffered a seizure and was told he had a brain tumor. His doctor said he would have to wait four and a half months for a brain scan to find out if it was cancerous. Unwilling to wait, he went to Buffalo, New York, where a magnetic resonance imaging (MRI) test showed a malignant tumor. McCreith paid $27,600 of his own money for surgery in Buffalo to remove the tumor. His local doctor said he would have probably waited eight months in Canada for this surgery.[26]

Some people use companies that help people find medical care outside of Canada. One such "medical broker," Douglas W. Hitchcock, formed the Free Trade Medical Network for that purpose. Hitchcock said, "We are very fortunate as Canadians to have the U.S. where the competitive marketplaces lets us cherry pick what we require without having to make the necessary investment in equipment."[27]

Canada and other nations that limit healthcare spending rely on the United States for innovations as well as supplemental care. If the United States nationalizes healthcare and limits payments for pharmaceuticals, the incentive for new medical developments is taken away. Public and private funding for research and development in the United States produces new medications, treatments, and technology that are used worldwide. If a single-payer insurer does not pay high enough prices for such innovations in equipment and pharmaceuticals, private companies will be unlikely to produce them. Public money for research might also be diminished if a government-run healthcare program required more money for administration in its budget.

Supporters of single-payer systems say that despite high levels of spending, Americans do not see corresponding benefits. They point to statistics that say Canadians have higher life expectancy and lower infant mortality rates than Americans. These misleading statistics do not consider other factors that affect longevity, such as lifestyles and genetics. The United States includes more diverse economic and ethnic groups than Canada and has higher crime rates. When statisticians adjust the numbers to remove people

QUOTABLE

Dr. Walter Kucharczyk, radiologist at Toronto Hospital

There's a black market [in Canada] for medicine. People who have influence in the ministry or friends at the hospital get different treatment.

Source: Elisabeth Rosenthal, "Canada's National Health Plan Gives Care to All, With Limits," *New York Times*, April 30, 1991. http://query.nytimes.com/gst/fullpage.html?res=9D0CE4 DB1030F933A05757C0A967958260&sec=health&spon=&pagewanted=all.

who die from accidents or crimes, Americans live as long or longer than people in other industrialized nations, including Canada. According to the Center for Medicine in the Public Interest, "While the overall life expectancy of Americans is lower than that of people [in] other nations, it [is] the result of higher rates of homicides, accidents, and obesity, factors that are at best tangentially related to the health care system."[28] Statistics also show that Americans who reach age 65 have a longer life expectancy than people in the Netherlands, for example, even though the average life expectancy at birth might be the same or lower for Americans.[29]

Analysts have compared Canada's single-payer system with systems that provide universal healthcare through different means, including a blend of private and public services. The Fraser Institute noted that of the 28 developed nations that offer universal access, Canada tied with Iceland as the "highest age-adjusted spender" but ranked near the bottom in terms of access to physicians and technology. The same report noted that two of the other countries achieved better health outcomes, five did not have significant waiting times, and two nations achieved both of these goals.[30] In all nine countries, private healthcare providers are permitted to deliver publicly funded care as well and all of them require people to contribute user fees to their care unless they are indigent. People are not banned from buying private insurance.

Some analysts believe the costs of healthcare delivery in Canada have been underestimated. How much do Canadians actually pay in taxes for their healthcare program? In his 1999 book *Code Blue*, Dr. David Gratzer calculated the total cost as 21 cents for every dollar earned—a total of $7,350 from an annual salary of $35,000.[31]

A single-payer system would not save as much money as supporters claim.

Advocates of a single-payer program say that America would save billions of dollars because the system would be more efficient and cost-effective. Many experts disagree, including economist Henry Aaron of the Brookings Institution in Washington, D.C., who said the costs of administering private insurance have been exaggerated and that a change to a single-payer system would most likely save less than predicted.[32]

Single-payer advocates tend to underestimate administrative costs. Single-payer plans are supposedly more efficient, but administration of such programs entails unexpected costs with the growth of government bureaucracy. Great Britain uses a single-payer system to administer its socialized National Health Service (NHS). A report in 2001 claimed that $7 billion was lost annually as a result of "waste, fraud, and inefficiency." This amounted to 20 percent of the healthcare budget and meant less funding for improvements designed to shorten waiting times, among other things.[33] An estimated $15 billion of the budget was lost due to "waste, mismanagement, incompetence and fraud" in 2004.[34] Critics of America's Medicare and Medicaid government programs say waste and fraud are ongoing problems for both.

The costs of funding a new national insurance program would not be simple and would likely require new taxes. Tax programs entail more administrative costs for government as legislators debate these issues and pass laws, which must then be administered by other departments in the government. Higher taxes for the healthcare system could hamper the overall economy as the government shifts more money to healthcare and taxpayers have less money to spend. Around the world, countries with universal health benefits have been struggling to fund social programs. Aging populations are raising the costs of both pensions and healthcare services, while the workforce paying taxes is smaller, due to lower birth rates in recent decades.

Summary

Single-payer systems produce government monopolies that abridge individual rights and do not always deliver what people need. Limits on annual healthcare spending are capped to fit budgetary requirements, and political decisions lead to rationing, which in turn means longer waits for healthcare services and less funding for healthcare facilities, technology, medical equipment, and innovation. Poor working conditions and personnel shortages can drive healthcare professionals to leave the system.

For these and other reasons, the American Medical Association (AMA), the nation's largest professional medical group, does not favor a single-payer plan. The AMA seeks to achieve universal insurance through free-market approaches that combine regulation of insurance companies, healthcare tax credits, and subsidies to help low-income people afford insurance. This kind of program maintains the competition that Americans need and would not require a massive overhaul of the current system.

Even if Americans were prepared to live with the myriad problems of a single-payer government monopoly, advocates of such a system must explain exactly how it would work. These advocates predict that all the needed funds would come from administrative savings, but many economists disagree. Citizens must therefore wonder how the money would be raised. Would employers pay taxes equal to what they now spend on employee health benefits? Would companies that do not currently offer health insurance pay into this system? At what rates would companies be taxed? What costs would individual Americans pay? How would the government help low-income families afford such charges? Would this new program encompass other government aid programs? What benefits would be provided for all? How would decisions be made to determine who gets rationed healthcare and what waiting times are "acceptable"?

Without clear and realistic answers to these questions, the nation would be unwise to adopt a single-payer program. When Canadians need care they cannot obtain in their own country, they cross the border. Where would Americans go for healthcare that was not available in a new national health monopoly?

Managed Care Systems Deliver Quality Healthcare

In 1969, John E. Wennberg, a physician and public health expert, and Alan Gittelsohn began studying medical practice patterns in various communities. As they gathered statistics relating to tonsillectomies (surgical removal of the tonsils) in different Vermont towns, these researchers were surprised to see vastly different rates. In one town, 20 percent of the children had their tonsils removed by age 15, while in a neighboring town with similar demographics, that figure was 70 percent.[1] The rates of other surgeries, such as appendectomies, showed similar differences in comparable towns. Did higher numbers of surgeries result from more medical need? On the contrary, Wennberg and Gittelsohn found that these differences reflected the number of physicians and specialists who were practicing in a given place. In towns with more surgeons, more surgeries were performed per capita. Patterns of hospital use likewise showed that supply tended to determine degree of use. When local hospitals had more beds of a certain type, people in that locale were more likely to be admitted to those units. Health outcomes did not seem to vary, however. In some cases, more treatment correlated with worse outcomes.

Other people were making similar observations. In 1974, a Senate subcommittee estimated that 2.4 million unnecessary surgeries were performed each year in the United States.[2] People noted high rates for hysterectomies (removal of a woman's reproductive organs), Caesarian sections (surgical deliveries of babies), and the use of high-tech diagnostic machines. Other studies showed that patients were being kept in hospitals based on when their insurance would run out, rather than medical need. A study by Allstate, released in 1984, concluded that about 30 percent of all medical costs came from fraud, duplication, abuse, or waste. This included unnecessary medications, treatment by specialists that could be done by others, hospitalization instead of outpatient care, and routine X-rays (costing more than $1 billion each year) that did not yield useful information for treatment.[3] Critics said that traditional medical practice, including "fee-for-service" payments from insurance and public programs, drove up costs without producing equal benefits. Doctors themselves noted overuse in medical practice, often springing from a desire not to deprive patients of any treatment that could help.

During these same years, federal and state government and employers became increasingly concerned about the soaring cost of health insurance. "Managed care" offered a promising solution. Supporters said this approach could bring more business efficiency to medicine, thus reducing costs while promoting competition based on quality and price.

Managed care organizations (MCOs), also called integrated delivery systems, have evolved into various forms. They include the health maintenance organization (HMO), preferred provider organization (PPO), and point of service plan (POS). MCOs use coordinated procedures for planning, financing, and delivering services. The insurer negotiates with providers to set fees. Some MCOs require patients to see only providers who belong to their system; others permit access to outside providers for additional fees. Some plans use prepayment methods, in which they pay providers a fee in advance for each person in the plan. Patients can enroll in an MCO either individually or with a group, usually through employment.

Early HMOs were group practices in the same healthcare facility. People paid a set fee to receive their healthcare from the group. When prepaid group practices emerged in the 1930s, they were controversial. Some medical societies, including the AMA, tried to have them declared illegal. In 1941, a court in the District of Columbia ruled that such a ban violated the Sherman Antitrust Act and was an unlawful restraint of trade. Nonetheless, some states continued to ban HMOs, even after the AMA voted in 1959 to stop opposing prepaid group practice plans.

During the early 1970s, government panels concluded that HMOs and other group systems could better control healthcare

THE LETTER OF THE LAW

The Sherman Antitrust Act (1890)
15 U.S.C. Section 1

The Sherman Antitrust Act was the first federal statute in the United States designed to limit business monopolies and cartels.

> Every contract, combination in the form of trust or otherwise, or conspiracy, in restraint of trade or commerce, or with foreign nations, is declared to be illegal. Every person who shall make any contract or engage in any combination or conspiracy hereby declared to be illegal shall be deemed guilty of a felony.

Source: http://www.usdoj.gov/atr/public/divisionmanual/chapter2.htm#_1_2.

costs and coordinate patient care. Enrollment in HMOs grew rapidly during the 1980s, increasing from 9.1 million in 1980 to 33.6 million in 1990.[4] By 1988, about 18 percent of all private insurance payments were going to HMOs. More preferred provider organizations were developing and negotiating with insurance companies to provide care. About 11 percent of all private insurance payments went to PPOs in 1988. By 1996, about 65 million Americans were enrolled in about 600 HMOs.[5] In 2001, 85 percent of all insured employees were in MCOs, not in traditional fee-for-service plans.[6]

Most Americans now receive healthcare coverage through some kind of MCO plan. Managed care offers a cost-effective way to reduce waste and inefficiency and provide coordinated care, especially in the area of prevention and chronic disease management. Routine care is often free or requires only a small copayment. Lower costs for insurance and care mean that more people can access services.

Managed care reduces costs associated with waste and overuse.

Numerous studies show that HMOs and other forms of managed care can reduce healthcare costs. A study conducted in 1996 found

THE LETTER OF THE LAW

The Health Maintenance Organization Act of 1973 (Public Law 93-222) 42 U.S.C. § 300

With strong support from President Richard M. Nixon, Congress passed the Health Maintenance Organization Act in 1973 to override the remaining state restrictions against these businesses. Under the HMO Act of 1973, companies that employ 25 or more people and are providing health insurance as an employee benefit are required to offer HMOs as an option to more conventional health plans.

that in large U.S. cities where most healthcare was provided by HMOs, the hospital costs were 11 percent lower than the national average and 19 percent lower than hospital costs in cities where most care was provided under fee-for-service arrangements.[7] Costs can be controlled by supervising providers, setting guidelines for patient care, covering certain services and products and excluding others, and monitoring cost-effectiveness as well as quality.

Managed care plans reduce costs by steering patients first to a physician known as the primary-care doctor, who can decide what further consultation or treatment is needed. This minimizes unnecessary, often expensive, trips to specialists. It can also reduce the number of unnecessary tests. Patients need an authorization for surgery, with a second opinion in some cases, and authorizations for hospital admission. More outpatient procedures also save costs, and many patients prefer outpatient surgery. Prepaid plans, or plans that pay physicians a set fee per patient, reduce the financial incentives to provide unnecessary care or treatments of dubious value. Coordination of care by one primary doctor also helps to prevent duplication of services that can occur when people visit different physicians on their own.

Critics say managed care focuses too much on saving money and not enough on individual patients. Money is, inevitably, part of the healthcare process because healthcare services involve financial transactions. Economic realities have become more compelling as healthcare costs rise each year, propelled by an aging population, more costly new treatments, and higher expectations from patients. Without effective cost controls, more people would lack access to healthcare services.

Besides, research continues to show that more care does not always mean better health. A recent study conducted by Dr. John Wennberg and his team showed that people over age 65 in Miami visited doctors much more often than their counterparts in Minneapolis. During their last six months of life, Miamians had six times more visits to specialists, spent twice as much time in hospitals, and were admitted to intensive care units (ICUs) more than twice as often as people in Minneapolis. Yet they did not have longer or healthier lives.[8]

Special concerns relate to spending for chronic illnesses and in the Medicare system, where about 30 to 35 percent of all funds are spent for people with chronic conditions during their last two years of life. A study from the Dartmouth Atlas Project, released in 2006, concluded that about one-third of all Medicare spending might be wasteful. Researchers looked at the records of 4.7 million Medicare patients from around the United States who died between 2000 and 2003. They found that hospitals that used more intensive treatments and spent more money on these patients did not achieve better health outcomes than hospitals that used fewer resources. In comparison with the healthcare system serving Salt Lake City, Utah (primarily Intermountain Healthcare), places that used more resources had worse outcomes. Donald M. Berwick, M.D., president of the Institute for Healthcare Improvement, said, "This report should end the 'more is better' myth in health care." Berwick noted that quality healthcare is possible at a lower cost once everyone involved in this process understands that fact. He also said, "new technologies and hospital stays can sometimes harm more than they help."[9]

The cost of treatment does not necessarily determine effectiveness either. Researcher Elliot S. Fisher found that Medicare patients with a similar age, socioeconomic status, and health status had a higher chance of dying within five years if they went to a high-spending hospital rather than a low-spending hospital.[10] One possible reason is that healthcare providers in those hospitals may ignore simple, routine care in favor of the high-tech and costlier treatments. In other studies, people who received treatment after a heart attack in a low-spending hospital had higher survival rates than those who went to a higher spending hospital.[11] People in managed care plans were found to have certain cancers (breast, cervical, colon, and melanoma) detected faster than people in more expensive conventional plans.[12]

Insurers must draw the line somewhere in order to focus on medically necessary care, but people are often unwilling to accept limits. Kaiser Permanente, one of the largest and oldest HMOs in the nation, faced such a situation in 1998 when it announced that it would not pay the cost of Viagra, a male erectile dysfunction drug, for its 9 million members. Kaiser said that Viagra is not a medical necessity. The company estimated that covering this drug would cost them $100 million a year and require them to raise insurance premiums. Kaiser further reasoned that erectile dysfunction is not life threatening and most members could afford to buy the drug themselves. Countries with universal health insurance reached a similar conclusion, classifying Viagra as a "lifestyle drug," not a health need, unless the man has a physical disease that causes impotence. State insurance regulators objected to Kaiser's decision and a male subscriber filed a lawsuit against the company. Kaiser applied to have the drug excluded from its list of covered prescriptions, but the California Department of Corporations, which oversees HMOs in California, refused to authorize this exclusion. In 2002, an appeals court in California agreed that Kaiser did not have the cover this drug.[13]

Managed care plans have also been attacked for not covering gastric bypass surgery for overweight people, yet some state regulators force them to cover it. MCO administrators have stated their reasons for excluding this procedure. The surgery is expensive (on average, $25,000). Complications can ensue, especially since overweight people tend to face higher risks with any surgery. Patients might require a great deal of follow-up care to deal with the changes in their digestive system. These costs can add up to $100,000 or more over a person's lifetime.[14]

In any case, supporters of managed care say these plans save healthcare dollars. In 1992, the Congressional Budget Office estimated the nation would spend $1.04 trillion on healthcare in 1995. That amount turned out to be $988 billion instead, and the savings were attributed largely to the use of managed care.[15]

In 2000, those savings were between $150 billion and $250 billion out of a total of $1 trillion in healthcare spending.[16] This benefits the overall U.S. economy. Without managed care, businesses and individuals would pay more for health insurance, and many employers would stop offering it. Government spending for public programs including Medicare, Medicaid, and SCHIP would be unsustainable.

Managed care can provide efficient and quality health services.

In the process of controlling costs, managed care can provide more coordinated healthcare. The primary-care physician assumes a central role in the treatment process. This doctor can monitor the patient's health status through the treatment process and access the patient's health history more easily. Doctor and patient can work together on preventive care, any acute conditions that arise, and especially chronic health problems, such as diabetes and high blood pressure. People with chronic conditions typically use the most healthcare services. The primary-care doctor can handle many issues alone and make referrals to specialists as needed. This can prevent the lack of coordination that results when people visit different specialists on their own without knowing what they need. In some cases, patients can even access the various services they need in one location, which enhances convenience.

Prevention is a major part of managed care, and MCO providers have strong incentives to keep people well. The MCO may remind people by mail or phone to schedule their routine care and age-related screenings. Some managed care programs encourage people to join health clubs or exercise programs to improve their health. MCOs have higher immunization rates than other insurance plans.[17]

Managed care plans aim to use hospitals only when necessary, which can make healthcare more efficient. Many people can, and would prefer to, receive treatment in an outpatient center, office, or their home. This not only saves costs but reduces the chance of complications and medical errors that can occur in hospitals. For example, the repair of an inguinal hernia once involved several days in a hospital. This surgery can now be done in an outpatient surgical center with local anesthesia, rather than general anesthesia under which patients are put to asleep. The outpatient procedure is not only cheaper but also less uncomfortable, and the chance of a recurrence is less than 0.01 percent as opposed to the previous rate of 10 percent.[18] Women are also spending less time in the hospital after giving birth. Instead of staying several days, they can be discharged within 24 to 36 hours if they have an uncomplicated vaginal delivery (true in about 70 percent of childbirths). This practice need not harm the health of mother or child, and new mothers often prefer to be home with their families.

MCOs have come up with innovative approaches to improve care while also saving on costs. Some operate health centers on nights and weekends where professionals can treat minor wounds and other minor acute situations faster than a typical emergency room. Patients and family members can learn how to handle certain situations on their own without professional expertise. In 1997, Optima Health, a division of Sentara Health Management in Virginia, implemented a program to help children learn to control their asthma-related symptoms. Children who took part in the program had fewer emergency room visits and hospitalizations.[19] Teams of nurses and doctors taught the children how to deal with symptoms and use a device that measures lung capacity. Some MCO staffs visit patients' homes before orthopedic surgery to help them prepare for an optimal postoperative recovery. Others operate childbirth education programs. MCOs also have been working to improve end-of-life care by collaborating with hospices.

Research does not confirm that people in managed care plans have worse health outcomes than people with traditional insurance.[20] Dr. David Jacobsen, a physician who works at an HMO and received his own cancer treatments there, writes, "I do not doubt that HMOs, like any other business, sometimes serve their customers poorly. But ... I have found that efficiency is perfectly compatible with compassionate, effective health care."[21]

A number of managed care organizations have received special praise for their performance. HMOs with high ratings include Group Health Cooperative of Puget Sound in Seattle, Washington, and Harvard Vanguard in Boston, Massachusetts. These plans involve one large medical group that can deliver well-coordinated care. When the School of Public Health in New York City conducted a four-year study of nonprofit medical and dental plans, it said that the Health Insurance Plan of Greater New York (HIP) gave the most complete contract for healthcare in the state. David Nash, an expert on HMOs, said, "Overwhelmingly, the published evidence supports the notion that quality of care in the managed care arenas equals, if not surpasses, the care in the private, fee-for-service sector."[22]

Critics say that MCOs reduce choices, but more choice is not necessarily better for patients. Some studies show better health outcomes with the group practice HMO model that includes a limited number of doctors. According to Nancy Kane, Ph.D., an expert on healthcare accounting and financing, "[T]he reality is that if you go to Vanguard [Harvard Vanguard Plan in Boston], where there is less choice, you are going to get better quality."[23]

Nancy Turnbull, a lecturer in the Harvard School of Public Health's Department of Health Policy and Management, notes that critics of managed care seem to assume things were much better decades ago, before MCOs were common. She says, "But I don't think that's true. . . . Not everybody did get care—and much of the care they did get was unnecessary."[24]

Managed care offers benefits to healthcare providers.

Critics say doctors, nurses, and other caregivers dislike managed care systems and frequently disagree with MCO administrators over treatment decisions, salaries and fees, record keeping, and other matters. While these problems can occur, they are often exaggerated.

Some healthcare providers appreciate their MCO affiliation and see some benefits with managed care, including clear standards for dealing with specific health problems. MCOs can provide physicians and hospitals with a steady group of patients. Hospitals that were struggling in previous decades have become financially sound based on arrangements with managed care plans. Nurses have seen benefits as well. It makes sense for skilled nurses and nurse practitioners with advanced training to perform some tasks that were previously assigned to physicians. This has expanded nurses' career opportunities and gives them more independent roles. Peter Buerhaus, a trained nurse and expert on economics of nursing, says that "ultimately there are no good substitutes for professional nurses. Registered nurses are a good buy for the money, and the market will reward them."[25] Working in a traditional HMO facility also offers healthcare providers more chances for professional collaboration than in a solo practice.

Because MCOs look for more efficient ways to deliver quality care, providers may have chances to develop innovative programs. Data collected from MCOs can yield information that points the way to better care, because they use sophisticated technology to track patients and services, which offers providers more ways to study health outcomes. As healthcare analyst David Mechanic writes, "Many of the structures of managed care offer the potential for developing a more evidence-based medical practice, a more thoughtful approach to decision making, and a more intelligent use of resources."[26]

Summary

Although MCOs have been accused of limiting people's choices and treatments, research has shown that *more* care does not always equal *better* care, or better health. Nor does more expensive care necessarily produce better outcomes. Since MCOs emerged and expanded, health outcomes in the United States have not worsened, and statistics show that MCOs have an impressive record in terms of health screenings and immunizations.

Negative incidents involving MCOs tend to grab news headlines, but few people hear about the quality care they deliver to large groups of people. MCOs differ in terms of the way they are organized, managed, and reimburse their providers, so criticisms of one do not necessarily apply to another. An entire system should not be blamed when individuals make mistakes. No method of healthcare delivery is completely free from error or misjudgments.

Because resources are not unlimited, tough choices must be made, especially when high costs threaten to leave many Americans uninsured. It is possible to deliver efficient and quality care within a reasonable budget. As MCOs evolve, issues are being resolved through internal improvements and government regulations that protect consumers. Government must be careful, though, not to impose unfair regulations on MCOs. For instance, a "Patients' Bill of Rights" bill, which was proposed in Congress in 2001, permitted patients to sue their HMOs for up to $5 million in pain and suffering as well as punitive damages. Such a bill would raise the costs of operating MCOs, leading to higher premiums for people who want health insurance and possibly forcing some companies out of business, leaving more people uninsured. Syd Gernstein, a research associate at the National Center for Public Policy Research, remarks, "HMOs are the most affordable source of health care for millions of Americans, so it is vital that HMO reformers not jeopardize their existence and affordability."[27]

Managed Care Systems Reduce Choices, Access, and Quality

In his 2007 documentary film *Sicko*, director Michael Moore interviewed Dawnelle Barris, whose daughter Mychelle died one night after an HMO did not authorize her treatment at a local emergency room. Barris called 911 the evening of May 6, 1993, because 18-month-old Mychelle had a high fever and was not breathing normally. Paramedics took the little girl to the nearest hospital emergency room, where her temperature was found to be an alarming 106.6 degrees. When medical staff contacted Barris's HMO for authorization, the ER doctor was authorized to give Mychelle breathing therapy. The ER doctor said Mychelle needed blood tests and probably antibiotics, but the HMO representative said that would be done at a hospital owned by the HMO and told Barris to drive her daughter there by car. During the next four hours, Barris and the ER doctor tried to convince the HMO representative that Mychelle was too sick to travel by car and needed immediate care, or at least an ambulance to the HMO's hospital. The representative refused. Meanwhile, Mychelle's condition deteriorated and she had a seizure. At that point, Kaiser agreed to an ambulance, but Mychelle went into cardiac arrest and died shortly after reaching the HMO hospital, which was located across town. An autopsy showed that Mychelle had a bacterial infection and could have survived if she had received antibiotics promptly at the first hospital.[1]

Tragedies like these arouse concerns about managed healthcare plans. To Dr. Linda Peeno, such cases are not surprising. Peeno is an outspoken critic of managed healthcare plans. During the 1980s, she worked for one of the nation's largest managed care companies, where she was responsible for approving or denying claims for payments. She became increasingly troubled that the company wanted her to deny claims in order to save money. Shortly after she saw the company install a $3.8 million sculpture in the rotunda of its headquarters, Peeno resigned. She later became a medical ethicist and testified before Congress in 1996 about problems in managed care systems.[2] In a 1998 article, Peeno recalled that "the pressure was always there to deny as much care as possible to cut costs—even if that meant pushing physicians toward some practices that endangered patients."[3]

Complaints abound from people who say their MCO refused to pay for tests, treatments, and medications. These complaints range from relatively minor inconveniences to serious lack of care. Patients and their families have also filed numerous lawsuits because of MCOs that refused life saving treatment. In one case, a California man died from cerebral hemorrhage (bleeding in his brain) after HMO had refused to authorize a CT scan of his brain when he complained of severe headaches.

The rise of managed care in the 1970s and 1980s can be traced mostly to employers and government officials who were dismayed by rising health insurance premiums. The people who envisioned managed care plans, many of them physicians, believed well-coordinated systems would provide quality healthcare without waste and duplication. The results have been disappointing as companies focused more on profits than people and intruded upon doctor-patient relationships. Though MCOs cite statistics showing their success with preventive care, they have been criticized for the way they respond to serious health needs, especially in times of emergency.

Managed care means fewer choices for healthcare consumers.

One big problem with managed care plans is the lack of choices for people enrolled in the plans. Since most people have job-linked insurance, employers choose their plans for them. These choices might reflect the employer's budgetary concerns more than the quality of care, even if it were possible to compare the quality of various plans.

One major tenet of the free market approach is that informed consumers make choices among competitive products. This does not work unless consumers have enough information to make sound judgments. Individuals and even companies may find it difficult to evaluate managed care plans, especially the fine print. The language in the plans can be confusing and may be designed to give the plan a positive spin. For example, health plans that offer limited choices may use the word "choice" in their name. According to Dr. Ivan J. Miller, this kind of deceptive language also applies to other things: "Cost-cutting programs are called 'quality improvement programs.' Gatekeepers, hired to divert patients from treatment, are called 'patient advocates.' . . . Such misleading language does not belong in health care."[4] Studies have shown that people who are poor and elderly have even more problems understanding how to use their managed care plans. MCOs differ in terms of the way they are organized, managed, and reimburse providers, which can make them difficult to compare.

Healthcare workers and doctors call for the adoption of a universal health-care system in the United States at the New York City premiere of Michael Moore's documentary, *Sicko,* on June 18, 2007.

These systems were also intended to foster more competition among healthcare services in terms of cost and quality, but that is not always possible either. In places with only one hospital, the hospital cannot compete with itself. Only 50 percent of Americans live in metropolitan areas with a high enough population to support two or three HMOs.[5] This means that one provider organization often monopolizes the areas with smaller populations. Moreover, since the 1990s many large managed care companies have merged so that fewer companies now control much more of the market. Smaller companies have found it difficult to compete because they have less negotiating power with doctors and other providers.

Once a person becomes part of managed care, the plan restricts other choices. People choose a primary-care doctor within the system. Then they encounter various "gatekeeping" procedures before they can visit specialists, be admitted to a hospital, or receive certain tests, outpatient procedures, and surgeries. Certain treatments and medications are covered by the plan; others are not. Copayments for services also apply in varying degrees.

Americans have long expressed concerns about the idea of government telling them which doctors or plans to use, or telling doctors how to treat patients. With managed care, the control shifts to employers and insurance companies, who limit healthcare choices to save money. Polls have shown that more people prefer traditional fee-for-service plans that offer more options than HMO plans. In one poll, 68 percent expressed that preference. Only 41 percent of people in managed care said they were "very confident" that their plan would pay for their treatment if they became seriously ill.[6]

MCOs give too much decision-making power to administrators and reviewers rather than clinicians.

One of the biggest concerns about MCOs is how treatment decisions are made. People must obtain authorization for various treatments their physicians think are indicated for their condition. Administrators far from the scene can determine clinical decisions. Often the physician must consult with a company employee who has less experience, education, and expertise with a particular health problem than the physician. These people might be healthcare professionals themselves, but some are not. Most importantly, these people have not seen the patient in question and cannot evaluate his or her condition.

Decision makers may rely on statistical charts and standardized guidelines for various clinical situations. These guidelines may work well in some healthcare situations, but they can fall short in an emergency, such as the case of Dawnelle Barris's daughter Mychelle.

Physicians may also face consequences for their spending choices. Some are subjected to reviews in which the MCO questions their choices and procedures. Formulas and lists are used to evaluate how well people are holding down costs.

Such practices can discourage physicians from working with MCOs, yet managed care is now so widespread that most physicians now work in the system. Physicians have resigned after deciding their MCO encouraged inadequate or substandard care and have even quit medicine entirely. Some who practice in lower-paid specialties, such as mental health, say that low fees make it difficult to cover expenses. In a study conducted by a group from Harvard University and Louis Harris and Associates, physicians in areas with higher concentrations of HMOs expressed more serious concerns about the quality of patient care and administrative practice issues than physicians in areas with less managed care.[7]

Cost-saving efforts in managed care can reduce both access and quality.

Companies have an incentive to limit spending because they keep the profits they make after paying the healthcare costs. The goal of profitability affects various aspects of the business, including the selection of subscribers. As David Mechanic points out, "strong incentives persist to market aggressively to the

QUOTABLE

Dr. Bruce Rushbaum, internal medicine practitioner

The [HMO] plans have swung so far against what is good for the patient and what is fair for the physician that it has impacted most negatively on the quality of healthcare in this country.

Source: "Doctors and Managed Care—Are HMOs Good Medicine?" Interview with CNN correspondent Charles Bierbauer, July 15, 1998. http://www.cnn.com/HEALTH/9807/15/hmo.docs.prognosis/.

most healthy and to avoid the highest-risk clients."[8] Critics say these plans clearly ration care, though none of these companies openly talk about rationing. According to Mechanic, "In truth, MCOs use a wide range of rationing strategies, including denial, deterrence, delay, and dilution of service."[9]

Deterrence and delay can occur when companies make it more difficult to obtain services. Complex administrative procedures and rules diminish access, which again saves money for the company. Some people give up as they try to negotiate the maze of gatekeepers and layers of bureaucracy. They may decide not to get the care after all, or to pay bills themselves when they do not understand their plan's regulations or cannot reach the right people to ask for help.

Critics say the system is set up to provide less care. Physicians in MCOs often have incentives to do less. When the MCO pays them a set monthly fee per patient, they may earn more money by seeing fewer patients and/or scheduling shorter visits. In that kind of system, a medical practice might earn just enough to cover expenses by seeing all the people who want services regularly each month. The MCOs also set standards for how long a visit should last—for example, 10 minutes for a routine pediatrics exam.

Company employees who decide whether or not to authorize services may receive bonuses for issuing denials. In *Mismanaged Care*, Michael E. Makover cites the case of a doctor working for a managed care company who told a surgeon she received a bonus of 10 percent of the cost of each procedure she could deny.[10]

The payment methods used in these systems may place economic risks on the providers. In some cases, payments are delayed or withheld. The MCO may stop working with doctors or hospitals that provide more treatment than they would like. Bonuses may also depend on how well doctors limit costs through using less treatment or not referring people to specialists. Providers on a fixed salary may have less incentive to limit treatments or the length of appointments, but what happens when MCOs penalize doctors for providing more services for individual patients with costly healthcare requirements? Dr. Ivan J. Miller writes that doctors may also be penalized for telling patients when they might benefit from a treatment that is not covered by their healthcare plan. This is called a "gag clause" and falls into a category called "managed care unfriendly" behavior.[11]

Standardized approaches can cause catastrophic results for individual patients. In his book *Health Against Wealth*, George Anders, a *Wall Street Journal* reporter, describes the case of a very sick, feverish baby whose parents were told to take him to a hospital 42 miles away. This hospital was part of their managed care plan and gave the company a discount in exchange for a certain amount of business. Furthermore, the person who handled their call (a nonphysician who had never seen their child) did not authorize the use of an ambulance. As the parents drove to the unfamiliar hospital that night in heavy rain, they passed three hospitals with good emergency facilities. They became lost and ended up at another hospital anyway. By then, their baby was much sicker and his heart stopped. He was resuscitated and treated, then moved to the hospital in the managed care plan, where he received around-the-clock care from several specialists for more than a week. His bacterial infection and the loss of blood flow that occurred during his heart attack caused such damage to his hands and feet that they had to be amputated.[12] The parents later sued the managed care company and a jury found the company guilty of medical negligence for not allowing the parents to have an ambulance take the baby to the hospital nearest their home for prompt treatment.[13]

Such an example shows what can happen when managed care decision makers adhere to strict rules designed to save on costs. Blind spots in the system can lead to tragic results. The true test of insurance comes when people are seriously ill, because that is the main reason people need insurance coverage.

Nurses have expressed concern about problems in managed care. In a 1996 survey of 5,000 registered nurses by the American Nurses Association (ANA), 90 percent said cost-saving measures lowered the safety and quality of patient care. Cuts in staff left fewer nurses caring for more patients, and nurses with less experience and fewer qualifications were being hired to replace higher-salaried nurses. In some hospitals, nurses said they were expected to not only care for more patients but also perform tasks that had once been performed by technicians and housekeeping personnel.[14] Like physicians, nurses have organized to oppose poor working conditions, and they have joined groups advocating stricter regulations for MCOs. Teri Britt, RN, MS, writes:

> The financial incentive in managed care is on not providing services and keeping as much of the capitation payment for reinvestment as possible. Short-term financial incentives provide significant areas of concern for policy makers, health care providers, and patients who yearn for long-term, high-quality solutions beyond the "bottom line." ... Nurses must be keenly aware of the underlying strategies and mechanisms in managed care in order to guard against poor patient care.[15]

Concerns about these kinds of problems led Congress to discuss a "Patients' Bill of Rights" that would apply to MCOs. President Bill Clinton supported such a bill during his administration (1993–2001), and the AMA has also supported it. Congress has continued to discuss new versions of the bill, which contain provisions that allow HMO members to seek emergency-room treatment at a facility that is not part of their insurance plan and also to sue their managed care insurer for malpractice when they are denied care. Democrats supported these provisions, but Republican opponents said the bill could increase the cost of health insurance. Although Congress had not passed the bill as of 2009, states have enacted their own bills to protect citizens.

Dr. Paul Ellwood was an early advocate of managed care and is credited with inventing the phrase "health-maintenance organization." In the late 1960s, Ellwood saw the chance for beneficial reforms in healthcare using an HMO model in which groups of physicians would meet people's annual needs for comprehensive healthcare in exchange for an annual prepayment. Ellwood later said that he thought the plans would compete with each other "on price and quality to serve informed consumers with the primary goal of enhancing health."[16] In 2001, Ellwood

---

THE LETTER OF THE LAW

New Jersey Consumer Bill of Rights
P.L. 1989, c. 170

New Jersey's Consumer Bill of Rights includes the following provisions to protect people covered by managed care plans:

The right to information on what health care services are covered and any limitations on that coverage.

The right to know how your carrier pays its doctors so you know if financial incentives or disincentives are tied to medical decisions.

The right to no "gag rules"—doctors are allowed to discuss all treatment options, even if they are not covered services.

The right to have a doctor—not an administrator—make the decision to deny or limit coverage of services.

The right to go to an emergency room without first contacting the carrier when it appears to a person that serious harm could result from not obtaining immediate medical treatment.

Source: State of New Jersey. Consumer Bill of Rights. http://www.nj.gov/dobi/lifehealthactuarial/hmo2008/billofrights.html.

expressed his disappointment with the way managed care had developed. He said, "The idea was to have health care organizations compete on price and quality. The form it took, driven by employers, is competition on price alone."[17]

Does managed care save as much money as supporters claim, and if so, who benefits? Author Michael Makover notes that these companies have made large profits, with overhead costs of around 30 percent.[18] By 1994, 10 managed care companies alone had $10.5 billion dollars in liquid assets. Makover writes, "The companies have taken credit for a trend [toward lower costs] that was already underway, and they have gutted the health care system for their own profit. The savings achieved have gone mostly to them, with only small savings and reduced quality of care for patients."[19]

MCOs include both nonprofit and for-profit facilities, but the majority are now for-profit facilities. For-profit MCOs with investors have even more reason to reduce costs, so researchers have wondered how this affects services. One study, reported in the *Journal of the American Medical Association (JAMA)* in 1999, looked at 329 HMO plans, including 248 investor-owned and 81 not-for-profit. The researchers found that investor-owned HMO plans had lower rates for 14 quality-of-care indicators, including annual eye examinations for diabetics, immunization, and mammography.[20]

Summary

MCOs may save money, although some experts dispute this idea, but to cut costs and earn profits, they ration care. These kinds of plans limit the choices of patients and healthcare providers, shift more burdens to the providers, and provide incentives to deliver less care. In some cases, the results have been fatal.

Though managed care advocates say these systems make insurance more widely available, the percentage of uninsured Americans has climbed since the 1980s, not decreased. Meanwhile, managed care businesses have amassed profits that enable them to pay large salaries to executives, and in the case of for-profit MCOs, shareholders. Profits also enable these companies to fund marketing campaigns and pay for lobbying efforts in Washington.

In recent decades, complaints from those who have suffered or lost loved ones because of managed care decisions have prompted federal and state legislators to consider various pieces of legislation to protect consumers. Several states have passed bills to guarantee certain rights, such as the ability to receive reimbursed care at the most convenient emergency room when necessary. Author George Anders concludes, "What the planners forget is that health care only seems like a vast industry ready to be conquered by statistical methods. Ultimately medicine is intensely personal; it is a service delivered one patient at a time."[21]

Other Topics for Debate

Americans continue to grapple with problems in healthcare, and reform is a perennial topic in political debates. As the previous chapters have shown, people disagree on certain core issues when it comes to healthcare funding and delivery. Debates attempt to define the roles and responsibilities of citizens, healthcare providers, insurers, and state and federal government in terms of sharing costs and benefits.

Free Market Versus Government Solutions?

Some Americans believe government is better suited to remedy problems in cost, quality, and access. Others say the free market should be allowed to operate with fewer restrictions, including much less government regulation. Observers note stark differences between these viewpoints: One side advocates improving the healthcare system by deregulating the insurance industry; the other side says the answer lies in more regulation.

Free-market advocates believe their approach reflects American political values of individual freedoms and sound economics. They advocate more competition and personal economic incentives as ways to lower healthcare costs and produce more satisfied consumers and providers. For those reasons, they support reforms that give individuals more funds to purchase their own insurance, such as tax credits and vouchers. They say this would work better than publicly funded programs like Medicaid, where the government pays healthcare providers on their behalf. This program does not always give people access to healthcare services because fees are so low. According to researchers Jonathan Gruber and Kosali Simon, "one-third of all physicians reported that they serve no Medicaid patients, and another third reported that they limit access of Medicaid patients in their practice."[1]

Free-market approaches include an end to employment-based health insurance. Critics say this system as unfair to people who are self-employed or do not obtain insurance at their job. The link between insurance and employment led to the rise of third-party payment for insurance, which was compounded during the 1960s with third-party payments through the government programs of Medicare and Medicaid. In both private and public insurance, people have sought more extensive benefits and used insurance to pay for routine healthcare. As a result, say critics, healthcare costs rose, and insurance was no longer used in the traditional way as protection against catastrophic events. Consumers also became less aware of how much services actually cost.

Free-market supporters have sought an end to publicly funded health programs and government mandates on insurance companies. Authors Lin Zinser and Paul Hsieh write:

By tying health insurance to employment through the income tax law—by providing preferential legal status and tax treatment to nonprofit companies and their payment plans for routine services—and by establishing government health insurance for the aged and poor in the form of Medicare and Medicaid, the government has created a system that violates individual rights and fosters an entitlement mentality.[2]

Zinser and Hsieh recommend that the current tax code be phased out over a period of two to three years in order to "treat all Americans equally with respect to how they purchase health insurance and medical services.[3]

Free-market advocates also object to laws that tell insurance companies what kinds of policies they can offer and what prices they can charge. Zinser and Hsieh write, "Insurance companies have a moral right to offer whatever policies and terms they deem marketable." These authors note that problems have occurred in states that imposed stricter mandates on insurance companies. In Kentucky, for instance, "forty-five of fifty insurers withdrew from the market there, which, in turn, led to fewer options and higher costs for consumers."[4] People who want less regulation say government mandates require insurance companies to cover too many services and also accept subscribers they do not want. These practices drive up costs, because companies must charge everyone more in order to cover mandated services. People who do not want extensive coverage are forced to pay more. Then, because people are paying for more, they want to get their money's worth. This provides an incentive to use more services.

Another proposal would let people buy insurance in any state. Some insurance companies might use this opportunity to move to states that impose fewer regulations regarding the extent of services they must cover in their policies.

Since new legislation was drafted in 2004, people have had the option of buying a high-deductible insurance policy with lower premiums and then taking an income tax deduction. That money can be put into a health savings account (HSA).

Free-market advocates supported this new program but say it does not go far enough to give people more options.

Opponents say free-market approaches do not reflect the realities of healthcare. In a true free market, consumers have enough information and power to negotiate with sellers. In the current system, the purchaser of the insurance is often an employer, not those who will use the services. The insurance company, not the patient, then pays for services. People in the system are also sometimes accountable to parties other than those they are treating. Doctors deal with insurers when they negotiate fees. Doctors who work for managed care companies can face conflicts of interest when they want to provide services the company does not want to fund. Insurance companies want to avoid enrolling people who are likely to need insurance the most. Managed care organizations want to pay for less care, not more, while the people they insure might want more care. Even when people buy their own insurance, they find it difficult to compare the "products" as they would when purchasing a car or TV set.

Healthcare expert Nancy Rhoden is among those who say that medical care is basically different from other purchases, and patients usually depend on the caregiver for advice and information. Rhoden writes:

> Consumers in the health care marketplace often get little chance to shop around, comparing price, effectiveness, etc. They may come in acutely ill and anxious; they may have had their discriminating powers affected by chronic mental or physical illness; they may know precious little about the "product" to be "consumed"; they may have denied the possibility of illness (and therefore not insured for it); and . . . some of them may be predictably affected by severe social, economic and educational advantages. No assumption should be allowed to mask these significant and sorrowful features of human existence.[5]

Economist Lester Thurow concludes:

Societies allow market mechanisms to work when buy-
ers are knowledgeable or willing to live with their mistakes and when society is willing to distribute goods and
services in accordance with the market distribution of
income. In the case of health care, neither of these two
necessary conditions exist.[6]

What about vouchers and health savings accounts? Critics
say these programs only work for people who have more money
and pay taxes, not the poor. With a pure market approach, huge
amounts of cash might be required to fund private insurance
for people who cannot afford it and those with extensive health
problems. Giving cash to people so they can buy insurance will
not work either if they use that money for other things.

Critics say that a free market in healthcare has given more
and more power to insurers, usually to large managed care
companies. As a result, financial considerations are a larger factor in the United States than in nations with more cooperative
national healthcare systems and less of a profit motive. On the
other hand, free-market advocates say that government has not
allowed the U.S. markets to operate properly and that government regulations and interference, not the free market, have
raised healthcare costs.

People who support government actions say government is
more likely to consider the public good than profit-oriented companies. They point to the U.S. Veterans Health Administration
(VHA) as proof that a government-run health program can be
cost-effective, efficient, and high quality. During the early 1990s,
the VHA was harshly criticized. Facilities were run-down and
people complained about poor care. The government considered dismantling the VHA but then decided to make improvements. These efforts succeeded, and the VHA has received high
praise for its performance in recent years. It outperformed

fee-for-service Medicare on all 11 measures of quality in a study conducted from 1997 and 1999. The nonprofit National Committee for Quality Assurance said that the VHA outperformed the nation's best-ranked hospitals in every category. Noting its success, author Shannon Brownlee writes, "The VHA manages such high levels of satisfaction and quality while taking care of a population that is older and sicker than the rest of the country."[7] She notes that this government-run system "doesn't have long lines; doesn't ration care; isn't filled with lazy, poorly trained doctors; and costs less per capita than our private system. The VHA even costs less per capita for its over sixty-five patients than Medicare."[8]

Some people prefer to combine free-market approaches with government action. This would include a private healthcare delivery system where the government would distribute vouchers to people who could not afford insurance but also restrict the kinds of plans insurers could offer. Blended approaches are used in other countries that have universal healthcare. The government sets certain standards for insurers that operate in the private market, and some governments insist that such companies be nonprofit. In Switzerland, everyone is insured and healthcare services are delivered privately. Everyone must buy a basic insurance policy, and the government helps those who cannot afford it. People who support this approach note that healthcare costs in Switzerland are 40 percent lower than in the United States, and the Swiss have not had problems with waiting lists or rationing of care. The French healthcare system has also been praised for covering all citizens and providing high-quality care without long waits. Private insurance companies are allowed to operate in France but, as in Switzerland, the government regulates companies so they do not make high profits.

Profit Or Nonprofit?

Should insurance companies make large profits on healthcare? Should pharmaceutical companies be able to make unlimited profits? How much profit is acceptable when it comes to health-care services? Americans have become increasingly concerned about high profits in healthcare, and some people think that ele-ment should be reduced, especially when it involves third-party payers. Others say the profit motive sparks excellence and new achievements. It may draw outstanding people to pursue health-care careers and encourage research and innovations in phar-maceuticals, medical equipment, and health-delivery industries. People note that the United States, with its profit-based system, has led the world in these areas.

As of 2009, the United States stood far above other nations in the size of its investor-owned healthcare sector. Dr. Arnold S. Relman is among those who find this troubling. He concludes that

> investor ownership of medical facilities has been a resounding failure, and ... the attempt to turn our [U.S.] system into a private commercial market is responsible for many of our current problems.... The United States has the most expensive health care system in the world, by far, and there is abundant evidence that the public does not get its money's worth.[9]

Dr. Lawrence Schneiderman notes that when healthcare businesses are responsible to stockholders, savings and profits go to people who have "nothing to do with health care." He says, "We are proud of being a free enterprise capitalist society that has produced many remarkable achievements, but we are trying to use that concept in health care, [building] health care on the profit-based market model and it's failing miserably."[10]

Some countries have concluded that profits do not belong in healthcare. In Switzerland, for example, insurance compa-nies are not allowed to make profits on basic coverage, which everyone is required to have. Swiss President Pascal Couchepin explained, "The idea is very simple: If it is a social insurance, and everybody is obliged to be a member of a health insurance system, you can't ask them to pay so that the shareholders get a better revenue."[11]

In a pure free-market setting, profits would not be controlled. Advocates of that approach say that free markets regulate these things naturally as supply and demand set prices. As the previous discussion showed, free-market advocates believe prices would decline if the government would stop regulating insurance companies, end the tax exemptions for employer-related health benefits, and terminate third-party payments for healthcare in the form of Medicare and Medicaid.

This situation, however, is not clear-cut. Both for-profit and nonprofit HMOs, for example, make money. A nonprofit company might use that money for building projects and employee pensions. A profit HMO might use extra cash for stock dividends or reserve funds it might need to pay out future claims. Yet supporters of nonprofit systems point to research showing that they provide better quality care. Arnold Relman notes that

> carefully controlled comparisons in the United States have shown [that] not-for-profit service is usually less expensive for the payers, and any differences in quality that can be demonstrated usually favor the nonprofits. Remember these are comparisons involving similar patients, similar communities, and institutions of similar size that provide similar services.[12]

In 2001, Dr. Paul Ellwood concluded that profit motives have come to dominate the managed care model he promoted during the 1970s. Ellwood remarked:

> I would ask if the for-profit model had subverted the objectives of health organizations to the point we need to insist the new model be not-for-profit firms. I find it disgusting when CEOs of leading managed care

organizations brag to Wall Street analysts that they have succeeded in raising premiums while lowering benefits.[13]

Choosing the Best Treatments

How do people decide which treatments are best? When is a treatment useful versus wasteful or even harmful? Determining effective treatments and setting appropriate standards are key aspects of healthcare debates, because they relate to quality, safety, and costs. These issues affect all the participants in healthcare, as well as legal cases that challenge a clinician's judgment. Using resources wisely means that more people can have access to care.

In recent decades, experts have been advocating the use of outcomes-based, also called evidence-based, medicine so that decisions are based on scientific evidence. In the past, new treatments have sometimes been adopted without research that verified their effectiveness. Institutions have not always known about programs at other institutions that effectively improved health outcomes or reduced medical errors.

As evidence-based medicine becomes increasingly available, caregivers will have more information to make treatment choices for optimal outcomes. New technology can disperse up-to-date information, such as standards from the Institute of Medicine that are designed to reduce medical error.

Supporters of evidence-based medicine say this approach can provide common ground for physicians, nurses, hospitals, patients, insurers, and government. It could reduce uncertainty about standards of care and help to set reasonable expectations. Such an approach can also reduce mistrust, dissatisfaction with treatment, and lawsuits.

Better care need not cost more and may even cost less. For instance, in New Hampshire, the Dartmouth-Hitchcock Medical Center worked on procedural standards for the care of people who had heart surgery. They surveyed physicians in their area and followed up with their patients. The use of these standards cut mortality rates by a rate of 24 percent between 1991 and 1996, while also cutting costs 20 percent and achieving high levels of patient and physician satisfaction.[14]

State-Based Universal Healthcare

Weary of waiting for healthcare reform from the federal government, some states have decided to develop their own universal system. Massachusetts has passed legislation that moves the state to universal coverage, and other states are making plans for programs that cover all of their citizens, or at least more.

State-sponsored health reform need not wait for national agreement on one type of plan. States can formulate plans based on local conditions and then organize financing and delivery systems that work for them. The federal government could set certain standards for state programs and allow states to use federal funds they now receive in ways that work to fund their approved programs. Smaller-scale programs on the state level can be implemented faster than a national program. They might also offer insights about what kinds of reforms work better than others.

Individual Responsibility for Health

As healthcare costs increase, especially for chronic illnesses, some people say the government should make Americans more accountable for their lifestyle choices. Some illnesses can be prevented by eating properly, exercising, being vaccinated against infectious diseases, and avoiding certain things: smoking, drinking in excess or taking illegal drugs, driving carelessly, and engaging in unsafe sexual activity. Health choices, especially in relation to diet, smoking, alcohol, and exercise, are said to contribute to six of the 10 leading causes of death in the United States: heart disease, stroke, cancer, diabetes, arteriosclerosis, and cirrhosis of the liver.[15] As of 2009, obesity was regarded as the number two cause of preventable death.[16] Without efforts to change these statistics, healthcare reform can only take the nation so far.

Of course, many illnesses and injuries are not preventable. Still, when individuals make poor health choices, society as a whole will pay, because costs and resources are shared, and taxes are used for public-health programs. People who make unwise choices can also threaten other people by driving while intoxicated or spreading STDs. Although people label these activities as "private," they have social consequences. Legislators consider this fact when they require people to wear seatbelts in cars and motorcycle helmets, for example.

Education and persuasion are the most common methods used to influence health decisions. Laws requiring nutritional information on food products were implemented to give people more information to make healthy choices. Incentives are also used, as when insurance companies offer discounts to people who do not smoke or who attend weight-loss clinics or exercise programs. People could also earn credits by taking part in programs that screen for diabetes, high blood pressure, and other conditions.

Health experts have debated if—and how—to hold people accountable if they choose certain actions. Critics who fear more government involvement warn about measures like taxing junk food or regulating the advertising of high-fat and high-sugar foods. They say that if government takes this path, it can invade people's privacy and lead to new unfair laws, such as taxing citizens who are not at their ideal weight.

Dr. Robert F. Meenan, a physician who has worked on programs to encourage better health habits, notes, "virtually all aspects of life style could be said to have an effect on the health of well-being of society." In an article for the *New England Journal of Medicine*, he wrote:

> Health professionals are trained to supply the individual with medical facts and opinions. However, they have no

personal attributes, knowledge, or training that qualifies them to dictate the preferences of others. Doctors ... find it hard to accept that some people may opt for a brief, intense existence full of unhealthy practices.[17]

Summary

There are no easy answers or quick solutions to the problems of cost, access, and quality in America's healthcare system. Disagreements reflect strongly held beliefs about how to best serve everyone involved. People on different sides of these debates support their positions with statistics, research studies, and expert opinions, as well as ethical, philosophical, economic, and political arguments. Will the United States build upon the current healthcare system or make dramatic changes in the years to come? The debate goes on.

Beginning Legal Research

The goals of each book in the POINT/COUNTERPOINT series are not only to give the reader a basic introduction to a controversial issue affecting society, but also to encourage the reader to explore the issue more fully. This Appendix is meant to serve as a guide to the reader in researching the current state of the law as well as exploring some of the public policy arguments as to why existing laws should be changed or new laws are needed.

Although some sources of law can be found primarily in law libraries, legal research has become much faster and more accessible with the advent of the Internet. This Appendix discusses some of the best starting points for free access to laws and court decisions, but surfing the Web will uncover endless additional sources of information. Before you can research the law, however, you must have a basic understanding of the American legal system.

The most important source of law in the United States is the Constitution. Originally enacted in 1787, the Constitution outlines the structure of our federal government, as well as setting limits on the types of laws that the federal government and state governments can enact. Through the centuries, a number of amendments have added to or changed the Constitution, most notably the first 10 amendments, which collectively are known as the "Bill of Rights" and which guarantee important civil liberties.

Reading the plain text of the Constitution provides little information. For example, the Constitution prohibits "unreasonable searches and seizures" by the police. To understand concepts in the Constitution, it is necessary to look to the decisions of the U.S. Supreme Court, which has the ultimate authority in interpreting the meaning of the Constitution. For example, the U.S. Supreme Court's 2001 decision in *Kyllo v. United States* held that scanning the outside of a person's house using a heat sensor to determine whether the person is growing marijuana is an unreasonable search—if it is done without first getting a search warrant from a judge. Each state also has its own constitution and a supreme court that is the ultimate authority on its meaning.

Also important are the written laws, or "statutes," passed by the U.S. Congress and the individual state legislatures. As with constitutional provisions, the U.S. Supreme Court and the state supreme courts are the ultimate authorities in interpreting the meaning of federal and state laws, respectively. However, the U.S. Supreme Court might find that a state law violates the U.S. Constitution, and a state supreme court might find that a state law violates either the state or U.S. Constitution.

Not every controversy reaches either the U.S. Supreme Court or the state supreme courts, however. Therefore, the decisions of other courts are also important. Trial courts hear evidence from both sides and make a decision, while appeals courts review the decisions made by trial courts. Sometimes rulings from appeals courts are appealed further to the U.S. Supreme Court or the state supreme courts.

Lawyers and courts refer to statutes and court decisions through a formal system of citations. Use of these citations reveals which court made the decision or which legislature passed the statute, and allows one to quickly locate the statute or court case online or in a law library. For example, the Supreme Court case *Brown v. Board of Education* has the legal citation 347 U.S. 483 (1954). At a law library, this 1954 decision can be found on page 483 of volume 347 of the U.S. Reports, which are the official collection of the Supreme Court's decisions. On the following page, you will find samples of all the major kinds of legal citation.

Finding sources of legal information on the Internet is relatively simple thanks to "portal" sites such as findlaw.com and lexisone.com, which allow the user to access a variety of constitutions, statutes, court opinions, law review articles, news articles, and other useful sources of information. For example, findlaw.com offers access to all Supreme Court decisions since 1893. Other useful sources of information include gpo.gov, which contains a complete copy of the U.S. Code, and thomas.loc.gov, which offers access to bills pending before Congress, as well as recently passed laws. Of course, the Internet changes every second of every day, so it is best to do some independent searching.

Of course, many people still do their research at law libraries, some of which are open to the public. For example, some state governments and universities offer the public access to their law collections. Law librarians can be of great assistance, as even experienced attorneys need help with legal research from time to time.

Common Citation Forms

Source of Law	Sample Citation	Notes
U.S. Supreme Court	*Employment Division v. Smith*, 485 U.S. 660 (1988)	The U.S. Reports is the official record of Supreme Court decisions. There is also an unofficial Supreme Court ("S. Ct.") reporter.
U.S. Court of Appeals	*United States v. Lambert*, 695 F.2d 536 (11th Cir.1983)	Appellate cases appear in the Federal Reporter, designated by "F." The 11th Circuit has jurisdiction in Alabama, Florida, and Georgia.
U.S. District Court	*Carillon Importers, Ltd. v. Frank Pesce Group, Inc.*, 913 F.Supp. 1559 (S.D.Fla.1996)	Federal trial-level decisions are reported in the Federal Supplement ("F. Supp."). Some states have multiple federal districts; this case originated in the Southern District of Florida.
U.S. Code	Thomas Jefferson Commemoration Commission Act, 36 U.S.C., §149 (2002)	Sometimes the popular names of legislation—names with which the public may be familiar—are included with the U.S. Code citation.
State Supreme Court	*Sterling v. Cupp*, 290 Ore. 611, 614, 625 P.2d 123, 126 (1981)	The Oregon Supreme Court decision is reported in both the state's reporter and the Pacific regional reporter.
State Statute	Pennsylvania Abortion Control Act of 1982, 18 Pa. Cons. Stat. 3203-3220 (1990)	States use many different citation formats for their statutes.

Cases

Maher v. Roe, 423 U.S. 464 (1977)

In this case, the U.S. Supreme Court ruled that the federal ban on funding elective abortions that are not medically necessary for women did not violate their rights to equal protection under the law, as guaranteed by the Fourteenth Amendment to the Constitution.

Harris v. McRae, 448 U.S. 297 (1980)

Cora McCrae, a resident of New York, sought to have Medicaid pay for her first trimester abortion. The U.S. Supreme Court ruled that states that take part in the Medicaid program, which provides health insurance for low-income people, are not required to fund elective abortions, even though they do provide funding for prenatal care and deliveries. This ruling upholds the Hyde Amendment.

Chaoulli v. Quebec, 1 S.C.R. 791 (2005)

A Canadian physician and his patient claimed that the Quebec government's health-insurance program failed to provide timely access to healthcare after the patient waited more than a year for hip-replacement surgery. The Supreme Court of Canada found that delays in the public healthcare system were widespread and serious: "The evidence also demonstrates that the prohibition against private health insurance and its consequence of denying people vital healthcare result in physical and psychological suffering that meets a threshold test of seriousness."

Statutes

Equal Protection Clause of the Fourteenth Amendment, U.S. Constitution (1868)

"No State shall make or enforce any law which shall abridge the privileges or immunities of citizens of the United States; nor shall any State deprive any person of life, liberty, or property, without due process of law; nor deny to any person within its jurisdiction the equal protection of the laws." This clause, enacted in 1868 shortly after the American Civil War ended, protected and promoted civil rights for former slaves.

The Sherman Antitrust Act (1890) 15 U.S.C. Section 1

This act states: "Every contract, combination in the form of trust or otherwise, or conspiracy, in restraint of trade or commerce, or with foreign nations, is declared to be illegal."

Hill-Burton Amendment (1946)

Enacted in 1946 as the Hospital Survey and Construction Act, Hill-Burton provided federal funds for healthcare facilities around the nation. By 1971, when the act was replaced with new legislation, funding from Hill-Burton increased hospital facilities by about 500,000 new beds and funded outpatient clinics, public-health centers, mental-health centers, and nursing homes.

Medicare Act (1965)

Created through an amendment to Title XIX of the Social Security Act of 1935, this program provides public-health insurance for Americans over age 65 and others who qualify under special circumstances.

Medicaid Act (1965)

This amendment to Title XIX of the Social Security Act of 1935 created a voluntary program in which states can receive federal funding to use with their own funds in providing medical insurance for the indigent.

Hyde Amendment (1976)

This amendment bars the use of federal funds to pay for abortions. Since many low-income women had been receiving abortions through the federal and state funded Medicaid program, opponents of this law say that this amendment prevents poor women from obtaining abortions.

Emergency Medical Treatment and Active Labor Act (EMTALA), 42 U.S.C. § 1395dd (1986)

This act required any hospital in the United States receiving funds from the Department of Human Services or from Medicaid and Medicare programs to treat any person in the emergency room or other suitable area of the hospital, regardless of their ability to pay or citizenship. Patients must be in a stable condition before they are released to their own care or another appropriate setting. This law applies to virtually all U.S. hospitals, and some institutions have been sued when they did not provide services.

Terms and Concepts

Entitlement

Evidence-based medicine

Fee-for-service

Health insurance

Health maintenance organization (HMO)

Managed care

Managed care organization (MCO)

Negative rights

Positive rights

Preexisting condition

Premium (insurance)

Public good

Single-payer insurance

Socialized medicine

Third-party payer

Underwriting

Introduction: Healthcare in the United States

1 Paul B. Ginsburg, Ph.D., "High and Rising Health Care Costs: Demystifying U.S. Health Care Spending," Research Synthesis Report no. 16, Robert Wood Johnson Foundation, October 2008, http://www.rwjf.org/files/research/101508.policysynthesis.costdrivers.rpt.pdf.

2 "Census: Fewer Americans Lack Health Insurance," CNNhealth.com, http://www.cnn.com/2008/HEALTH/08/26/census.uninsured/index.html. See also: C. DeNavas-Walt, B. D. Proctor, and J. Smith, "Income, Poverty, and Health Insurance Coverage in the United States: 2007," U.S. Census Bureau, August 2008.

3 Commonwealth Fund Commission on a High Performance Health System, "Why Not the Best?: Results from a National Scorecard on U.S. Health System Performance," Commonwealth Fund, 2008, p. 12.

4 Laurence J. Kotlikoff, *The Healthcare Fix: Universal Insurance for All Americans.* Cambridge: MIT Press, 2007, pp. 7–8.

5 National Coalition on Health Care, "Health Insurance Costs: Facts on the Cost of Health Insurance and Health Care," http://www.nchc.org/facts/cost.shtml.

6 Ibid.

7 Sara Lubbes, "Study: Health Care Costs Threaten American Businesses in Global Economy," *Congressional Quarterly Politics,* May 9, 2008, http://www.commonwealthfund.org/Content/Newsletters/Washington-Health-Policy-in-Review/2008/May/Washington-Health-Policy-Week-in-Review---May-12--2008/Study--Health-Care-Costs-Threaten-American-Businesses-in-Global-Economy.aspx. See also: U.S. Census Bureau, "Health Insurance Coverage Status and Type of Coverage by Sex, Race, and Hispanic Origin: 1999 to 2007," http://www.census.gov/hhes/www/hlthins/historic/hihistt1.xls. Elise Gould, "The Erosion of Employer-Sponsored Health Insurance," EPI Briefing Paper no. 223, Economic Policy Institute, October 9, 2008, p. 1; http://epi.3cdn.net/d1b4356d96c21c91d1_ilm6b5dua.pdf.

8 Morgan Malveon, Karen Davenport, and Ellen-Marie Whelan, "High-Risk Insurance Pools: A Flawed Model for Reform," Center for American Progress, September 29, 2008, http://www.americanprogress.org/issues/2008/09/flawed_model.html.

9 American College of Physicians (ACP), "Achieving a U.S. Health Care System That Is Second to None: Why Settle for Anything Less?" January 31, 2008, http://www.acponline.org/advocacy/events/state_of_healthcare/snhcbrief2008.pdf.

10 Peter J. Cunningham, "Trade-Offs Getting Tougher: Problems Paying Medical Bills Increase for U.S. Families, 2003–2007," Center for Studying Health System Change, September 2008, http://www.hschange.org/CONTENT/1017.

11 Ibid.

12 "Medical Bills Leading Cause of Bankruptcy, Harvard Study Finds," ConsumerAffairs.com, February 3, 2005, http://www.consumeraffairs.com/news04/2005/bankruptcy_study.html.

13 Ibid.

14 John Carreyrou, "As Medical Costs Soar, the Insured Face Huge Tab," *Wall Street Journal,* November 29, 2007, http://online.wsj.com/public/article_print/SB119610495315004214.html.

15 See: Ed Kashi and Julie Winokur, *Denied: The Crisis of America's Uninsured.* Montclair, N.J.: Talking Eyes Media, 2003.

16 National Coalition on Health Care, "Health Insurance Costs: Facts on the Cost of Health Insurance and Health Care," http://www.nchc.org/facts/cost.shtml.

17 David R. Francis, "Healthcare Costs Are Up. Here Are the Culprits," *Christian Science Monitor,* December 15, 2003, http://www.csmonitor.com/2003/1215/p21s01-coop.html.

18 Michael Carter, "Diagnosis: Mismanagement of Resources," *OR/MS Today,* April 2002, http://www.lionhrtpub.com/orms/orms-4-02/frmismanagement.html.

19 "Health Insurance Costs: Facts on the Cost of Health Insurance and Health Care," National Coalition on Health

Care, http://www.nchc.org/facts/cost.
shtml.

20 Henry J. Aaron and Joseph P. Newhouse,
"Meeting the Dilemma of Health Care
Access: Extending Insurance Coverage
while Controlling Costs," in Michael E.
O'Hanlon, ed., *Opportunity 08: Indepen-
dent Ideas for America's Next President.*
Washington, D.C.: Brookings Institution
Press, 2007, p. 278.

21 Francis, "Healthcare Costs Are Up."

22 Sarah Burd-Sharps and Kristen Lewis,
et al., *The Measure of America: American
Human Development Report, 2008-2009.*
New York: Social Science Research
Council and Columbia University Press,
2008.

23 Commonwealth Fund, "Why Not the
Best?" p. 10.

24 Ibid, p. 4.

25 The Commonwealth Fund Commission
on a High Performance Health
Care System, "Why Not the Best?
Results from a National Scorecard
on U.S. Health System Performance,"
September 2006, p. 10, http://www.
commonwealthfund.org/usr_doc/
Commission_whynotthebest_951.
pdf#nameddest=table.

26 Robert H. LeBow, M.D., *Health Care
Meltdown: Confronting the Myths and
Fixing Our System.* Chambersburg, Pa.:
A. C. Hood, 2003, p. 3.

27 Centers for Disease Control and Prevention, *Health, United States, 2007.* Hyatts-
ville, Md.: U.S. Department of Health
and Human Services, National Center
for Health Statistics, 2007, p. 227, http://
www.cdc.gov/nchs/data/hus/hus07.
pdf#027.

28 John E. Murray, *Origins of American
Health Insurance: A History of Industrial
Sickness Funds.* New Haven, Conn.: Yale
University Press, 2007, p. 74.

29 *Source Book of Health Insurance Data,
1980–81.* Washington, D.C.: Health
Insurance Association of America, p. 12.

30 Cited in United States Congress. Joint
Economic Committee. Subcommittee
on Education and Health. *Health-care
Reform: How to Push Less Paper and
Treat More Patients: Hearings Before
the Subcommittee on Education and
Health of the Joint Economic Committee,*

*Congress of the United States, 102nd
Congress, 2nd session, October 2, 16,
and 30, and December 9, 1991.* U.S.
Government Printing Office, 1992, p.
146.

31 Tom Daschle, et al., *Critical: What We
Can Do About the Health-Care Crisis.*
New York: Thomas Dunne Books, 2008,
p. 53.

32 Stephen J. Whitfield, *The Culture of the
Cold War.* Baltimore: Johns Hopkins
University Press, 1991, p. 23.

33 U.S. Census Bureau: Poverty, http://
www.census.gov/hhes/www/poverty/
histpov/hstpov2.html.

34 Barbara L. Wolfe, "Reform of Health
Care for the Nonelderly Poor," in Sheldon H. Danziger, Gary D. Sandefur, and
Daniel H. Weinberg, eds., *Confronting
Poverty: Prescriptions for Change.* Cambridge, Mass.: Harvard University Press,
1994, p. 265.

35 Joseph A. Califano Jr., *America's Health
Care Revolution: Who Lives? Who Dies?
Who Pays?* New York: Random House,
1986, p. 55.

36 Ibid., p. 58.

37 Sheila Smith, et al., "National Health
Projections Through 2008," *Health Care
Financing Review,* http://www.cms.
hhs.gov/HealthCareFinancingReview/
Downloads/99winterpg211.pdf.

38 Ibid.

39 Ibid.

40 "Coverage & Access: About One in
Nine U.S. Children Uninsured in 2007,
Study Finds," Kaiser Daily Health Policy
Report, November 26, 2008, http://
www.kaisernetwork.org/Daily_Reports/
rep_index.cfm?DR_ID=55779.

41 Kotlikoff, *Healthcare Fix,* p. 8.

42 Lisa Potetz, "Financing Medicare: An
Issue Brief," Henry J. Kaiser Family
Foundation, January 2008, http://www.
kff.org/medicare/upload/7731.pdf.

43 Kevin Sack and Katie Zezima, "Growing Need for Medicaid Strains States,"
New York Times, Jan. 21, 2009,
http://www.nytimes.com/2009/01/22/
us/22medicaid.html.

44 Employee Benefit Research Institute,
"2007 Health Confidence Survey: Rising Health Care Costs Are Changing
the Way Americans Use the Health

Care System," EBRI Notes, November 2007, http://www.ebri.org/publications/notes/index.cfm?fa=notesDisp&content_id=3857.

45 "Critics: Healthcare System Fails in Many Ways," ABC News, October 15, 2006, http://abcnews.go.com/print?id=2570911.

46 Laurene A. Graig, *Health of Nations: An International Perspective on U.S. Health Care Reform*, 3rd ed. Washington, D.C.: Congressional Quarterly Press, 1999, p. 10.

Point: Healthcare Is a Basic Human Right

1 Transcript of second presidential debate at CNN.com: http://www.cnn.com/2008/POLITICS/10/07/presidential.debate.transcript/.

2 Norman Daniels, "Equal Opportunity and Health Care Rights for the Elderly," in Thomas J. Bole 3rd and William B. Bondeson, eds., *Rights to Health Care*. Dordrecht; Boston: Kluwer Academic, 1991, p. 205.

3 President's Commission for the Study of Ethical Problems in Medicine and Biomedical and Behavioral Research, An Ethical Framework for Securing Access to Health Care. Washington, D.C.: U.S. Government Printing Office, 1983, p. 29.

4 Universal Declaration of Human Rights, http://www.un.org/Overview/rights.html.

5 International Covenant on Economic, Social, and Cultural Rights (ICCPR), http://www.unhchr.ch/html/menu3/b/a_cescr.htm.

6 Ibid.

7 American Declaration of the Rights and Duties of Man (1948), Article XI, http://www.oas.org/juridico/English/ga-Res98/Eres1591.htm.

8 Inter-American Court of Human Rights, Annual Report 1984-5, Resolution No. 12/85, Case No. 7615 (1985) at Resolutions Paragraph 3(a), (c).

9 International Labour Organization, Resolution Concerning Health Care as a Basic Human Right. Joint Meeting on Social Dialogue in the Health Services: Institutions, Capacity and Effectiveness; October 2002, Geneva, http://www.

ilo.org/public/english/dialogue/sector/techmeet/jmhs02/jmhs-res.pdf.

10 Roemer, Milton Irwin. *National Health Systems of the World*, vol. 1 New York: Oxford University Press, 1991.

11 Interview with Lawrence Schneiderman, M.D., "On Ethics and Medicine," *Healthwise*, May 2001, p. 5.

12 Diane Rowland and Catherine Hoffman, "The Impact of Health Insurance Coverage on Health Disparities in the United States," Human Development Report Office, 2005.

13 For more discussion, see Brian D. Smedley, Adrienne Y. Stith, and Alan R. Nelson, eds., *Unequal Treatment: Confronting Racial and Ethnic Disparities in Health Care*. Washington, D.C.: National Academy Press, 2003.

14 American Human Development Index report, http://measureofamerica.org/wp-content/uploads/2008/07/ahdr-exec-summ.pdf.

15 Jean Carmalt and Sarah Zaidi, Center for Economic and Social Rights, October 2004, p. ii, http://cesr.org/filestore2/download/733/health%20report%20final%20on%20website%20(oct%2028).pdf.

16 President's Commission for the Study of Ethical Problems in Medicine and Biomedical and Behavioral Research, An Ethical Framework for Securing Access to Health Care. Washington, D.C.: U.S. Government Printing Office, March 1983, p. 29.

17 Jesse Jackson Jr., "Building a New Wall: The Fundamental Right to Healthcare," Huffington Post, November 26, 2008, http://www.huffingtonpost.com/rep-jesse-jackson-jr/building-a-new-wall-the-f_b_146606.html.

18 Special Message to the Congress Recommending a Comprehensive Health Program, November 19, 1945. Cited in Alan Derickson, *Health Security for All: Dreams of Universal Health Care in America*. Baltimore: Johns Hopkins University Press, 2005, p. 93.

19 Quoted in Robert Dallek, *Lyndon B. Johnson: Portrait of a President*. New York: Oxford University Press, 2004, pp. 196–197.

20 Derickson, *Health Security*, p. 139.

21 Quoted in Malcolm L. Johnson (ed.), *The Cambridge Handbook of Age and Ageing*. Cambridge, UK: Cambridge University Press, 2005, p. 227.

22 United States Conference of Catholic Bishops, http://www.faithfulreform.org/index.php/Theology-and-Policy/United-States-Conference-of-Catholic-Bishops.html.

23 Ibid.

24 "Statement of Rabbi David Saperstein, Religious Action Center of Reform Judaism National Coalition on Health Care," January 23, 1997, http://rac.org/Articles/index.cfm?id=462&pge_prg_id=9169.

25 "Health Care Access Resolution—House Concurrent Resolution 99," April 30, 2002, http://www.kaisernetwork.org/health_cast/uploaded_files/Transcript_HealthTogether.pdf.

26 Quoted in John Canham-Clyne, *The Rational Option for a National Health Program*. Stony Creek, Conn.: Pamphleteer's Press, 1995, p. 34.

27 "Nation's Health Care System Ill, Survey Finds," Community Voices: Healthcare for the Underserved, http://www.communityvoices.org/Article.aspx?ID=298.

28 Opinion Research Corporation, "Americans & Health Care Reform: How Access and Affordability Are Shaping Views," September 14, 2004; pp. 13–14, http://www.civilsocietyinstitute.org/reports/RFA%20CSI%20Healthcare%20FINAL.pdf.

29 Aaron Blake, "Poll Shows Many Republicans Favor Universal Healthcare, Gays in Military," The Hill, June 28, 2007, http://thehill.com/campaign-2008/poll-shows-many-republicans-favor-universal-healthcare-gays-in-military-2007-06-28.html.

30 Ibid.

31 Dr. Gro Harlem Brundtland, "The Need for Improved Global Health: Duty or Opportunity?" Speech given at BioVision, World Life Sciences Forum, February 8, 2001, http://www.who.int/director-general/speeches/2001/english/20010208_biovision.en.html.

32 Derickson, *Health Security*, p. 165.

33 Norman Solomon, "Warfare and Healthcare," FAIR: Fairness & Accuracy in Reporting, March 11, 2008, http://www.fair.org/index.php?page=3312.

34 Quoted in "Critics: Healthcare System Fails in Many Ways," ABC News, October 15, 2006, http://abcnews.go.com/print?id=2570911.

35 "Election 2008/Republican Candidates Discuss Health Care, Other Issues Related to Hispanics During Debate," Kaiser Daily Health Policy Report, December 10, 2007, http://www.kaisernetwork.org/daily_reports/health2008dr.cfm?DR_ID=49306.

36 Quoted in Richard A. Epstein, *Mortal Peril: Our Inalienable Right to Health Care?* Reading, Mass: Addison-Wesley Pub. Co., 1997, p. 29.

37 Miller Center of Public Affairs and MacNeil-Lehrer Productions. Debate: "Resolved: Americans have a fundamental right to health care, and it is the obligation of government to secure that right," April 9, 2008, http://millercenter.org/public/debates/healthcare.

Counterpoint: Healthcare Is a Marketplace Commodity That People Can Buy and Sell

1 Sheldon Richman, "Perspective: The Right to Medical Care," *The Freeman*, September 1, 1997, http://www.thefreemanonline.org/departments/perspective-the-right-to-medical-care/.

2 Michael Burton, Ph.D., "'Right' to Health Care Violates Individual Rights," *Cascade Commentary* (Oregon), May 2006, no. 2006-6, http://www.cascadepolicy.org/pdf/health_ss/2006_06.pdf.

3 Leonard Peikoff, "Health Care Is Not a Right." Speech delivered December 1993, reprinted in *Capitalism*, January 23, 1998, http://www.capmag.com/article.asp?ID=9.

4 For discussion, see Carolyn L. Engelhard and Arthur Garson Jr., "The Right to Health Care and the Role of Government in Public Policy," Miller Center of Public Affairs (University of Virginia): White Paper, http://webstorage3.mcpa.virginia.edu/debates/whitepaper/deb_2008_0409_healthcare.pdf.

5 *Maher v. Roe* 423 U.S. 464 (1977)

6 Epstein, *Mortal Peril*, p. 4.

7 Scott McPherson, "Health-Care Social-ism," *Freedom Daily*, June 2003, http://www.fff.org/freedom/fd0306e.asp.

8 Bole, *Rights to Health Care*, p. 2.

9 Peikoff, "Health Care Is Not a Right."

10 Michael Hurd, "Rhetoric Notwithstanding, Health Care Is Not a Right," *Washington Times*, April 6, 1993; http://www.drhurd.com/medialink/health-care-not-a-right.html.

11 Richard A. Epstein, *Mortal Peril*, p. 2.

12 Thomas Halper, "Rights, Reforms, and the Health Care Crisis: Problems and Prospects," in Bole, *Rights to Health Care*, p. 138.

13 Carolyn L. Engelhard and Arthur Garson Jr., "The Right to Health Care and the Role of Government in Health Policy," p. 2, http://webstorage3.mcpa.virginia.edu/debates/whitepaper/deb_2008_0409_healthcare.pdf.

14 Halper in Bole, *Rights to Health Care*, p. 137.

15 Joseph Newhouse and the Insurance Experiment Group, *Free for All?: Lessons from the RAND Health Insurance Experiment*. Cambridge, Mass.: Harvard University Press, 1993, p. 243.

16 Halper in Bole, *Rights to Health Care*, p. 138.

17 Burton, "'Right' to Health Care."

Point: The United States Should Adopt a National Single-Payer Healthcare System

1 T. R. Reid, "Taiwan Takes the Fast Track to Universal Health Care," National Public Radio, *All Things Considered*, April 15, 2008, http://www.npr.org/templates/story/story.php?storyId=89651916).

2 Ibid.

3 Ibid.

4 Associated Press/Yahoo Poll, December 14–20, 2007. Results reported in Associated Press, "Poll Highlights: The Rules of Attraction," http://news.yahoo.com/page/election-2008-political-pulse-voter-worries-highlights

5 Institute of Medicine's Committee on the Consequences of Uninsurance, *Hidden Costs, Values Lost: Uninsurance in America*. Washington, D.C.: National Academy Press, 2003, p. 5.

6 Quoted in Rebecca Cook Dube, "Canada Inches Toward Private Medicine," *Christian Science Monitor*, August 8, 2005, http://www.csmonitor.com/2005/0808/p06s01-woam.html.

7 Lisa Girion and Michael A. Hiltzik, "An Eroding Model for Health Insurance," *Los Angeles Times*, October 21, 2008, http://www.latimes.com/features/health/policy/la-fi-insure21-2008,oct21,0,3739128.story?page=4.

8 Steffie Woolhandler, M.D., et al., "Costs of Health Care Administration in the United States and Canada," *New England Journal of Medicine*, August 21, 2003, http://content.nejm.org/cgi/content/short/349/8/768.

9 Robert Chernomas and Ardeshir Sepehri, *How to Choose?: A Comparison of the U.S. and Canadian Health Care Systems*. Amityville, N.Y.: Baywood Pub. Co., 1998, p. 105.

10 "USA Wastes More on Health Care Bureaucracy Than It Would Cost to Provide Health Care to All of the Uninsured," Medical News Today, May 28, 2004, http://www.medicalnewstoday.com/articles/8800.php Study: http://www.citizen.org/publications/release.cfm?ID=7271.

11 Physicians for a National Health Program (PNHP). Single-Payer National Health Insurance." http://www.pnhp.org/facts/single_payer_resources.php.

12 Daniel J. Costello, Lisa Girion, and Michael A. Hiltzik, "The Battle of the Medical Bills," *Los Angeles Times*, Oct. 23, 2008, http://articles.latimes.com/2008/oct/23/business/fi-insure23.

13 Steffie Woolhandler et. al. "Costs of Health Care Administration in the United States and Canada," *New England Journal of Medicine*, August 21, 2003, p. 678, http://content.nejm.org/cgi/content/full/349/8/768.

14 Donald L. Barlett and James B. Steele, *Critical Condition: How Health Care in America Became Big Business—and Bad Medicine*. New York: Broadway Books, 2005, p. 238.

15 Costello, et al, "The Battle of the Medical Bills."

16. "Special Report: CEO Compensation," Forbes.com, April 21, 2005, http://www.

forbes.com/static/pvp2005/LIRRI3M.
html.

17. "Special Report: CEO Compensation,"
Forbes.com, April 21, 2005, http://
www.forbes.com/static/execpay2005/
LIRS5NI.html?passListId=12&passYear
=2005&passListType=Person&uniqueId
=S5NI&datatype=Person.

18 Solomon, "Warfare and Healthcare."

19 Thomas W. O'Rourke and Nicholas
K. Iammarino, "Future of Healthcare
Reform in the USA: Lessons From
Abroad." Presented at the annual
meeting of the American Association
for Health Education, March 23, 2000,
http://www.mdanderson.org/pdf/
niammarino-futurereform-article.pdf.

20 Paul Krugman, "One Nation Uninsured," *New York Times*, June 13, 2005,
http://www.nytimes.com/2005/06/13/
opinion/13krugman.html.

21 Lewin Group Technical Assessment of
Four Health Proposals, August 20, 2007,
http://healthcareforallcolorado.org/pdfs/
BriefOverview5Proposals.pdf.

22 Interview with Uwe Reinhardt and
Tsung-mei Cheng, "Sick Around
the World," *Frontline*, November
10, 2007, http://www.pbs.org/wgbh/
pages/frontline/sickaroundtheworld/
interviews/reinhardt.html.

23 Costello, et al, "The Battle of the Medical Bills."

24 Hiltzik, et. al, "The Battle Over Bills," A-
1.

25 Stacey Burling, "American College
of Physicians Endorse Single-Payer,"
Philadelphia Inquirer, December 4,
2007, http://www.commondreams.org/
archive/2007/12/04/5604.

26 "US Doctors Support Universal Health
Care–Survey," Reuters, March 31,
2008, http://www.reuters.com/article/
latestCrisis/idUSN31432035.

27 "Senate Floor Statement of Senator
Max Baucus Regarding Health Care and
Competitiveness," Senate Committee on
Finance, July 25, 2005, http://finance.
senate.gov/press/Bpress/2005press/
prb072505a.pdf.

28 Christopher Tarver Robertson, et al.,
"Get Sick, Get Out: The Medical Causes
of Home Mortgage Foreclosures,"
Health Matrix, August 2008, p. 87,

http://www.pnhp.org/news/2008/
october/medical_causes_of_ho.php.

29 RealtyTrac, http://www.realtytrac.com/
foreclosure/foreclosure-rates.html.

30 "Indepth: Health Care: Introduction,"
CBCNews.ca, August 22, 2006,
http://www.cbc.ca/news/background/
healthcare/.

31 Ibid.

32 Nadeem Esmail and Maureen Hazel
with Michael Walker, "Waiting Your
Turn: Hospital Waiting Lists in Canada,
2008 Report," Fraser Institute, October
2008, http://www.fraserinstitute.
org/commerce.web/product_files/
WaitingYourTurn2008.pdf.

33 James Arvantes, "Canadian Physician
Exodus Benefits United States,
Hurts Canada." Aafp News Now,
May 2, 2007, http://www.aafp.
org/online/en/home/publications/
news/news-now/professional-issues/
20070502canadiandocs.html.

34 "Indepth: Health Care: The Ruling: In
Reaction." CBCNews.ca, Feb. 16, 2006,
http://www.cbc.ca/news/background/
healthcare/ruling_reaction.html.

35 Dr. Colleen M. Flood and Meghan
McMahon, "Privatized Medical Care
No Cure for Waiting Lists," *The Star*
(Toronto), September 18, 2007, http://
www.thestar.com/printArticle/257556.

36 Ronald J. Glasser, M.D., "The Doctor
Is Not In: On the Managed Failure of
Managed Health Care," *Harper's*, March
1998, p. 35.

37 "Emergency Room Delays" (editorial),
New York Times, January 19, 2008,
http://www.nytimes.com/2008/01/19/
opinion/19sat3.html.

38 Interview with Linda Peeno, M.D.,
"Health Talk: Break Down of Health
Care," *Washington Post*, May 21, 2002,
http://discuss.washingtonpost.com/wp-
srv/zforum/02/health052102.htm.

39 Ibid.

40 Susan Rosenthal, M.D., "The U.S.
and Canada: Two Models of Medical
Rationing," June 27, 2007, http://
susanrosenthal.com/articles/the-us-
and-canada-two-models-of-medical-
rationing.

41 Canham-Clyne, *Rational Option*, p. 47.

42 "HealthCare access Resolution–House Concurrent Resolution 99", April 30, 2002, http://www.pnhp.org/news/2002/may/healthcare_access_re.php.

43 Karen Davis, et al., "Medicare vs. Private Insurance: Rhetoric and Reality," Commonwealth Fund, October 1, 2002, http://www.commonwealthfund.org/publications/publications_show.htm?doc_id=221504.

44 Quoted in "Health Outcomes Often Better in Canada Than U.S.–Review," CBCNews.ca, April 18, 2007, http://www.cbc.ca/health/story/2007/04/18/health-canada-us.html.

45 Canham-Clyne, *Rational Option*, p. 91.

Counterpoint: The United States Should Not Adopt a National Single-Payer Healthcare System

1 Quoted in Barlett and Steele, *Critical Condition*, p. 238.

2 Michael Bliss, "Health Care Without Hindrance: Medicare and the Canadian Identity," in David Gratzer, M.D., ed., *Better Medicine: Reforming Canadian Health Care*. Toronto: ECW Press, 2002, p. 41.

3 Barbara Sibbald, "RN=Really Neglected, Angry Nurses Say," *Canadian Medical Association Journal (CMAJ)*, April 16, 1999, http://www.cmaj.ca/cgi/reprint/160/10/1490.pdf. See also David Spurgeon, "Quebec Nurses Enter Third Week of Strike," *British Medical Journal (BMJ)*, July 17, 1999, p. 144, http://www.pubmedcentral.nih.gov/articlerender.fcgi?artid=1116265. "Doctors on Strike in Newfoundland," CBC News Canada. October 2, 2002, http://www.cbc.ca/canada/story/2002/10/01/nflddoctors021001.html.

4 "Saskatchewan Health-Care Workers Set to Escalate Strike," CBCNews.ca, September 23, 2002, http://www.cbc.ca/canada/story/2002/09/23/sask_health020923.html.

5 *Chaoulli v. Quebec* [2005] 1 S.C.R. 791

6 Ibid.

7 Interview with Pascal Couchepin, "Sick Around the World," *Frontline*, November 10, 2007, http://www.pbs.org/wgbh/pages/frontline/sickaroundtheworld/interviews/couchepin.html.

8 Nadeem Esmail and Michael A. Walker, "How Good Is Canadian Health Care?" Fraser Institute, p. 57, http://www.fraserinstitute.org/commerce.web/product_files/HowGoodisCanadianHealthCare2008.pdf.

9 Ibid.

10 Ibid.

11 Michael P. Coleman, et al., "Cancer Survival in Five Continents: A Worldwide Population-Based Study," *Lancet Oncology*, vol. 9, issue 8, August 2008, pp. 730–756.

12 Nadeem Esmail and Michael A. Walker with Margaret Bank, "Waiting Your Turn: Hospital Waiting Lists in Canada, 2007," Fraser Institute, http://www.fraserinstitute.org/Commerce.Web/product_files/WaitingYourTurn2007.pdf.

13 Ibid.

14 Esmail, et al., *Waiting Your Turn 2008*.

15 "Wait Times for Surgery, Medical Treatments At All Time Highs: Report," CBCNews.ca, October 15, 2007, http://www.cbc.ca/health/story/2007/10/15/fraser-report.html.

16 Danylo Hawaleshka, "Family Physicians Fed Up With Job Pressures," *MacLean's*, December 8, 2003, http://www.thecanadianencyclopedia.com/index.cfm?PgNm=TCE&Params=M1ARTM0012542.

17 "Canadian Doctors Overworked, Unable to Meet Patients' Needs: Survey," CBCNews.ca, January 9, 2008, http://www.cbc.ca/health/story/2008/01/09/doctors-survey.html.

18 Cal Gutlin, M.D., "Family Medicine in Canada: Vision for the Future," *CFP-MFC Journal*, February 10, 2005, http://www.pubmedcentral.nih.gov/articlerender.fcgi?artid=1472980.

19 Quoted in "Canadian Doctors Overworked, Unable to Meet Patients' Needs: Survey."

20 Kevin C. Fleming, M.D., "High-Priced Pain: What to Expect From a Single-Payer Health Care System," Heritage Foundation, Sept. 22, 2006, http://www.heritage.org/Research/healthcare/bg1973.cfm.

21 Arvantes, "Canadian Physician Exodus Benefits United States, Hurts Canada."

22 Clifford Krauss, "Windsor Journal; Doctors Eying the U.S.: Canada Is Sick About It," *New York Times*, Oct 17, 2003, http://query.nytimes.com/gst/fullpage.html?res=980CE0DE143EF934A25753C1A9659C8B63.

23 Maureen Hazel and Nadeem Esmail, "Leaving Canada for Medical Care," *Fraser Forum*, December 2008, http://am.eri.ca/Commerce.Web/product_files/LeavingCanadaforMedicalCare.pdf.

24 Quoted in Anthony DePalma, "Doctor, What's the Prognosis? A Crisis for Canada," *New York Times*, December 15, 1996, http://query.nytimes.com/gst/fullpage.html?res=9E0CE1DB133EF936A25751C1A960958260&sec=health&spon=&pagewanted=all.

25 Quoted in Rebecca Cook Dube, "Canada Inches Toward Private Medicine," *Christian Science Monitor*, August 8, 2005, http://www.csmonitor.com/2005/0808/p06s01-woam.html.

26 Canadian Constitution Foundation news release on *McCreith & Holmes v. Ontario*, May 2, 2007, http://www.canadianconstitutionfoundation.ca/files/pdf/newsrelease-05-02-2007.pdf.

27 Quoted in DePalma, "Doctor, What's the Prognosis? A Crisis for Canada."

28 Center for Medicine in the Public Interest, "Learn the Facts: Life Expectancy," BigGov Health, http://www.biggovhealth.org/resource/myths-facts/life-expectancy/.

29 Ibid.

30 Nadeem Esmail, "Kill the Canada Health Act," *National Post*, May 7, 2004, http://www.fraserinstitute.org/Commerce.web/article_details.aspx?pubID=3468.

31 David Gratzer, M.D., *Code Blue: Reviving Canada's Health Care System*. Toronto:ECW Press, 1999, pp. 175, 178.

32 Henry J. Aaron, "The Costs of Health Care Administration in the United States and Canada—Questionable Answers to a Questionable Question," *New England Journal of Medicine*, vol. 349, no. 8, August 21, 2003, pp. 801–803.

33 Rosie Waterhouse and David Cracknell, "Fraud and Waste Cost NHS 7 Billion Pounds a Year," *Sunday Times* (London), December 2, 2001.

34 Fair Investment Company, "Howard Slams Brown's 'Credit Card' Budget," March 17, 2004. Cited in Fleming, "High-Priced Pain."

Point: Managed Care Systems Deliver Quality Healthcare

1 Phillip Longman, *Best Care Anywhere: Why VA Care Is Better Than Yours*. Sausalito, Calif.: PoliPointPress, 2007, p. 85.

2 Michael L. Millenson, *Demanding Medical Excellence: Doctors and Accountability in the Information Age*. Chicago: University of Chicago Press, 1997, p. 166.

3 Califano, *America's Health Care Revolution*, p. 6. See also: Shannon Brownlee, *Overtreated: Why Too Much Medicine Is Making Us Sicker and Poorer*. New York: Bloomsbury, 2007.

4 David Dranove, *The Economic Evolution of American Health Care: From Marcus Welby to Managed Care*. Princeton, N.J.: Princeton University Press, 2002, p. 67.

5 Tufts Managed Care Institute, "A Brief History of Managed Care," http://63.251.142.241/downloads/BriefHist.pdf.

6 Christine Gorman, "Playing the HMO Game," *Time*, June 24, 2001, http://www.time.com/time/magazine/article/0,9171,139532,00.html.

7 CRS Reports, "Managed Health Care: A Primer." CRS Reports for Congress. September 30, 1997, pp. 11-12. Data from: KPMG Peat Marwick. *The Impact of Managed Care on U.S. Markets, Executive Summary*, 1996, http://www.law.umaryland.edu/marshall/crsreports/crsdocuments/97-913_EPW.pdf.

8 Gina Kolata, "More May Not Mean Better in Health Care, Studies Find," *New York Times*, July 21, 2002, http://query.nytimes.com/gst/fullpage.html?sec=health&res=9D00E6D91638F932A15754C0A9649C8B63.

9 Quoted in John E. Wennberg, Elliot S. Fisher, et al., Dartmouth Atlas Project of Health Care, *The Care of Patients with Severe Chronic Illness: An Online Report on the Medicare Program*. Lebanon, N.H.: Trustees of Dartmouth College, 2006, http://www.dartmouthatlas.org/press/2006_atlas_press_release.shtm.

10 Longman, *Best Care Anywhere*, p. 86.

11 Ibid.

12 Susan Brink, "HMOs Were the Right Rx," *U.S. News and World Report*, March 1, 1998, http://www.usnews.com/usnews/biztech/articles/980309/archive_003420_3.htm.

13 *Kaiser Foundation Health Plan, Inc. v. Zingale*, 121 Cal. Rptr. 2nd 741, 749 (Cal Ct. App. 2002).

14 Benjamin M. Craig and Daniel S. Tseng, "Cost-Effectiveness of Gastric Bypass Surgery for Severe Obesity," *American Journal of Medicine*, vol. 113, no. 6, 2002, pp. 491–498.

15 Brink, "HMOs Were the Right Rx."

16 Ibid.

17 Lauren Randel, et al. "How Managed Care Can Be Ethical," *Health Affairs*, July/August 2001, http://content.healthaffairs.org/cgi/content/full/20/4/43.

18 David Jacobsen, "Cost-Conscious Care: In Praise of HMOs," *Reason*, June 1996, http://www.reason.com/news/show/29946.html.

19 The Center for Managing Chronic Disease, "Asthma Health Outcomes Project," December 2007, http://asthma.umich.edu/media/ahop_autogen/AHOP_2-21-08.pdf.

20 Quoted in Peter Wehrwein, "Picking Through the Pieces," *Harvard Public Health Review*, Summer 1999, http://www.hsph.harvard.edu/review/summer_picking.shtml.

21 Jacobsen, "Cost-Conscious Care."

22 Quoted in David Jacobsen, "Cost-Conscious Care."

23 Quoted in Wehrwein, "Picking Through the Pieces."

24 Ibid.

25 Ibid.

26 David Mechanic, "A Balanced Framework for Change," *Journal of Health Politics, Policy and Law*, October 1999, pp. 1107–1114, http://muse.jhu.edu/journals/journal_of_health_politics_policy_and_law/v024/24.5mechanic.html.

27 Syd Gernstein, "Patients' Bill of Rights Could Provide Patients With a Bigger Health Care Bill," *National Policy Analysis*, no. 348, July 2001, http://www.nationalcenter.org/NPA348.html.

Counterpoint: Managed Care Systems Reduce Choices, Access, and Quality

1 *Dawnelle Barris, et al., etc. v. County of Los Angeles, et al.* Superior Court of the State of California for Los Angeles, Case No. TC, 007062.

2 See: Linda Peeno, M.D., "Managed Care Ethics: The Close View." Prepared for U.S. House of Representatives Committee on Commerce, Subcommittee on Health and Environment, May 30, 1996, http://www.nomanagedcare.org/DrPeenotestimony.html.

3 Linda Peeno, M.D., "A Voice for Elizabeth," *Reader's Digest*, August 1998, pp. 150–151.

4 Ivan J. Miller, "Eleven Unethical Managed Care Practices Every Patient Should Know About," *Independent Practitioner*, Spring 2005.

5 Canham-Clyne, *Rational Option*, p. 30.

6 TIME/CNN poll of 1,024 Americans in June 2001, in Gorman, "Playing the HMO Game."

7 Karen Donelan, et al., "The New Medical Marketplace: Physicians' Views," *Health Affairs*, September/October 1997, vol. 16, no. 5, p. 147, http://content.healthaffairs.org/cgi/reprint/16/5/139.pdf.

8 David Mechanic. See also: Rudolf Klein et al., *Managing Scarcity: Priority Setting and Rationing in the National Health Service*. Philadelphia: Open University Press, 1996.

9 Ibid.

10 Michael E. Makover, *Mismanaged Care: How Corporate Medicine Jeopardizes Your Health*. Amherst, N.Y.: Prometheus Books, 1998, p. 95.

11 Miller, "Eleven Unethical Managed Care Practices."

12 George Anders, *Health Against Wealth: HMOs and the Breakdown of Medical Trust*. Boston: Houghton Mifflin, 1996, pp. 1–5.

13 *James Don Adams, Jr. and Lamona K. Adams, et al. v. Kaiser Foundation Health Plan of Georgia, Inc.* State Court of Fulton County, Ga., C.A.F. 93VS79895 (1995).

14 Robert Pear, "Stakes High as California Debates Ballot Issues to Rein In H.M.O.s," *New York Times*, October 3,

1996, http://query.nytimes.com/gst/fullpage.html?res=9B03E6D6173FF930A35753C1A960958260&sec=health&spon=&pagewanted=all.

15 Teri Britt, "Managed Care and Managing Risks," *Nursing World*, 2001, http://www.nursingworld.org/mods/archive/mod312/cerm302.htm#Porter.

16 Paul M. Ellwood Jr., "Does Managed Care Need to Be Replaced?" Presentation to the Graduate School of Management, University of California, Irvine, October 2, 2001, http://www.medscape.com/viewarticle/408185.

17 Quoted in Gorman, "Playing the HMO Game."

18 Makover, p. 97.

19 Ibid, p. 98.

20 David U. Himmelstein, et al., "Quality of Care in Investor-Owned vs. Not-for-Profit HMOs," *Journal of the American Medical Association*, 282, No. 2, 1999, pp. 159–163.

21 Anders, *Health Against Wealth*, p. 14.

Conclusion: Other Topics for Debate

1 Quoted in Greg D'Angelo, "Health Care Tax Credits: The Best Way to Advance Affordability, Choice, and Coverage," WebMemo no. 1711. Heritage Foundation, November 28, 2007, http://www.heritage.org/Research/healthcare/wm1711.cfm.

2 Lin Zinser and Paul Hsieh, "Moral Health Care vs. 'Universal Health Care,'" *Objective Standard*, vol. 2, no. 4, Winter 2007, http://www.theobjectivestandard.com/issues/2007-winter/moral-vs-universal-health-care.asp.

3 Ibid.

4 Ibid.

5 Nancy Rhoden, "Free Markets, Consumer Choice, and the Poor: Some Reasons for Caution," in Bole, p. 220.

6 Lester Thurow, "Learning to Say 'No,'" *New England Journal of Medicine*, vol. 311, no. 24, 1984, p. 1571.

7 Brownlee, *Overtreated*, p. 270.

8 Ibid, p. 271.

9 Arnold Relman, "Market-Based Health Care in the United States and Its Lessons for Canada," in Bruce Campbell and Greg Marchildon, eds., *Medicare: Facts, Myths, Problems, and Promise.* Toronto: James Lorimer & Co., 2007, p. 91.

10 Schneiderman interview, "On Ethics and Medicine," p. 5.

11 Couchepin interview.

12 Relman, in *Medicare*, p. 93.

13 Paul M. Ellwood Jr., "Does Managed Care Need to Be Replaced?" http://www.medscape.com/viewarticle/408185.

14 Gorman, "Playing the HMO Game."

15 Califano, *America's Health Care Revolution*, p. 71.

16 Ali H. Mokdad, et al., "Actual Causes of Death in the United States, 2000," *Journal of the American Medical Association*, vol. 291, no. 10, March 10, 2004, http://jama.ama-assn.org/cgi/content/abstract/291/10/1238.

17 Robert F. Meenan, "Improving the Public's Health: Some Further Reflections," *New England Journal of Medicine*, vol. 294, no. 1, Jan. 1, 1976, pp. 45–46.

RESOURCES ⫸

Books

Barlett, Donald L., and James B. Steele. *Critical Condition: How Health Care in America Became Big Business—and Bad Medicine.* Garden City, N.J.: Doubleday, 2004.

Bayer, Ronald, et al. *Public Health Ethics.* New York: Oxford University Press, 2007.

Brownlee, Shannon. *Overtreated: Why Too Much Medicine Is Making Us Sicker and Poorer.* New York: Bloomsbury, 2007.

Burd-Sharps, Sarah, Kristen Lewis, et al. *The Measure of America: American Human Development Report, 2008-2009.* New York: Social Science Research Council and Columbia University Press, 2008.

Campbell, Bruce, and Greg Marchildon, eds. *Medicare: Facts, Myths, Problems, and Promise.* Toronto: James Lorimer & Co., 2007.

Daschle, Tom, et al. *Critical: What We Can Do About the Health-Care Crisis.* New York: Thomas Dunne Books, 2008.

Derickson, Alan. *Health Security for All: Dreams of Universal Health Care for All Americans.* Baltimore: Johns Hopkins University Press, 2005.

Dranove, David. *The Economic Evolution of American Health Care: From Marcus Welby to Managed Care.* Princeton, N.J.: Princeton University Press, 2002.

Dranove, David. *What's Your Life Worth?: Health Care Rationing—Who Lives? Who Dies? Who Decides?* Upper Saddle River, N.J.: F.T. Prentice Hall, 2003.

Funigiello, Philip J. *Chronic Politics: Health Care Security from FDR to George W. Bush.* Lawrence: University Press of Kansas, 2005.

Graig, Laurene A. *Health of Nations: An International Perspective on U.S. Health Care Reform,* third ed. Washington, D.C.: Congressional Quarterly Press, 1999.

Gratzer, David, M.D., ed. *Better Medicine: Reforming Canadian Health Care.* Toronto: ECW Press, 2002.

Gratzer, David, M.D. *Code Blue: Reviving Canada's Health Care System.* Toronto: ECW Press, 1999.

Kashi, Ed, and Julie Winokur. *Denied: The Crisis of America's Uninsured.* Montclair, N.J.: Talking Eyes Media, 2003.

Kotlikoff, Laurence J. *The Healthcare Fix: Universal Insurance for All Americans.* Cambridge, Mass.: MIT Press, 2007.

LeBow, Robert H., M.D. *Health Care Meltdown: Confronting the Myths and Fixing Our System.* Chambersburg, Pa.: A. C. Hood, 2003.

Longman, Philip. *Best Care Anywhere: Why VA Care Is Better Than Yours.* Sausalito, Calif.: PoliPoint Press, 2007.

Murray, John E. *Origins of American Health Insurance: A History of Industrial Sickness Funds.* New Haven, Conn.: Yale University Press, 2007.

O'Hanlon, Michael E., ed. *Opportunity 08: Independent Ideas for America's Next President.* Washington, D.C.: Brookings Institution Press, 2007.

Quadagno, Jill. *One Nation Uninsured: Why the United States Has No National Health Insurance.* New York: Oxford University Press, 2005.

Relman, Arnold S., M.D. *A Second Opinion: Rescuing America's Health Care.* New York: PublicAffairs, 2007.

Richmond, Julius B., and Rashi Fein, Ph.D. *The Health Care Mess: How We Got Into It and What It Will Take to Get Out.* Cambridge, Mass.: Harvard University Press, 2005.

Articles and Reports

Blake, Aaron. "Poll Shows Many Republicans Favor Universal Healthcare, Gays in Military." The Hill, June 28, 2007. Available online. URL: http://thehill.com/campaign-2008/poll-shows-many-republicans-favor-universal-healthcare-gays-in-military-2007-06-28.html.

Brundtland, Gro Harlem, M.D. "The Need for Improved Global Health: Duty or Opportunity?" Speech given at BioVision, World Life Sciences Forum. February 8, 2001. Available online. URL: http://www.who.int/director-general/speeches/2001/english/20010208_biovision.en.html.

Burton, Michael, Ph.D. "'Right' to Health Care Violates Individual Rights." *Cascade Commentary* (Oregon). May 2006, no. 2006-6. Available online. URL: http://www.cascadepolicy.org/pdf/health_ss/2006_06.pdf.

Carmalt, Jean, and Sarah Zaidi. *The Right to Health in the United States of America: What Does It Mean?* Center for Economic and Social Rights. October 2004. p. ii–iii. Available online. URL: http://cesr.org/filestore2/download/733/health%20report%20final%20on%20website%20(oct%2028).pdf.

Carreyrou, John. "As Medical Costs Soar, the Insured Face Huge Tab." *Wall Street Journal.* November 29, 2007.

Carter, Michael. "Diagnosis: Mismanagement of Resources." *OR/MS Today.* April 2002. Available online. URL: http://www.lionhrtpub.com/orms/orms-4-02/frmismanagement.html.

Commonwealth Fund Commission on a High Performance Health System. "Why Not the Best? Results from a National Scorecard on U.S. Health System Performance." Commonwealth Fund, 2008. Available online. URL: http://www.acponline.org/advocacy/events/state_of_healthcare/snhcbrief2008.pdf.

Cunningham, Peter J. "Trade-Offs Getting Tougher: Problems Paying Medical Bills Increase for U.S. Families, 2003–2007." Center for Studying Health System Change–HSC. September 2008. Available online. URL: http://www.hschange.org/CONTENT/1017.

D'Angelo, Greg. "Health Care Tax Credits: The Best Way to Advance Affordability, Choice, and Coverage." WebMemo no. 1711 (Heritage Foundation), November 28, 2007. Available online. URL: http://www.heritage.org/Research/healthcare/wm1711.cfm.

DeNavas, Walt, C. B. Procter, and J. Smith. "Income, Poverty, and Health Insurance Coverage in the United States: 2007." U.S. Census Bureau, August 2008.

Donelan, Karen, et al. "The New Medical Marketplace: Physicians' Views." *Health Affairs,* September/October 1997, vol. 16, no. 5, pp. 139–148.

Ellwood, Paul M., Jr. "Does Managed Care Need to Be Replaced?" Presentation to the Graduate School of Management, University of California–Irvine, October 2, 2001. Available online. URL: http://www.medscape.com/viewarticle/408185.

Engelhard, Carolyn L., and Arthur Garson Jr. "The Right to Health Care and the Role of Government in Public Policy." Miller Center of Public Affairs (University of Virginia) white paper. Available online. URL: http://

webstorage3.mcpa.virginia.edu/debates/whitepaper/deb_2008_0409_
healthcare.pdf.

Francis, David R. "Healthcare Costs Are Up. Here Are the Culprits." *Christian Science Monitor*. December 15, 2003. Available online. URL: http://www.csmonitor.com/2003/1215/p21s01-coop.html.

Gernstein, Syd. "Patients' Bill of Rights Could Provide Patients With a Bigger Health Care Bill." *National Policy Analysis*, no. 348. Available online. URL: http://www.nationalcenter.org/NPA348.html.

Ginsburg, Paul B., Ph.D. "High and Rising Health Care Costs: Demystifying U.S. Health Care Spending." Research Synthesis Report no. 16, Robert Wood Johnson Foundation, October 2008. Available online. URL: http://www.rwjf.org/files/research/101508.policysynthesis.costdrivers.rpt.pdf.

Gorman, Christine. "Playing the HMO Game." *Time*. June 24, 2001. Available online. URL: http://www.time.com/time/magazine/article/0,9171,139532,00.html.

Gould, Elise. "The Erosion of Employer-Sponsored Health Insurance." EPI Briefing Paper no. 223, Economic Policy Institute, October 9, 2008, p. 1. Available online. URL: http://epi.3cdn.net/d1b4356d96c21c91d1_ilm6b5dua.pdf.

Himmelstein, David U., et al. "Quality of Care in Investor-Owned vs. Not-for-Profit HMOs." *Journal of the American Medical Association*, 282, no. 2, 1999, pp. 159–163.

Kolata, Gina. "More May Not Mean Better In Health Care, Studies Find." *New York Times*. July 21, 2002. Available online. URL: http://query.nytimes.com/gst/fullpage.html?sec=health&res=9D00E6D91638F932A15754C0A9649C8B63.

Lubbes, Sara. "Study: Health Care Costs Threaten American Businesses in Global Economy." *Congressional Quarterly Politics*, May 9, 2008. Available online. URL: http://www.cqpolitics.com.

Malveon, Morgan, and Karen Davenport and Ellen-Marie Whelan. "High-Risk Insurance Pools: A Flawed Model for Reform." Center for American Progress, September 29, 2008. Available online. URL: http://www.americanprogress.org/issues/2008/09/flawed_model.html.

"Medical Bills Leading Cause of Bankruptcy, Harvard Study Finds." ConsumerAffairs.com, February 3, 2005. Available online. URL: http://www.consumeraffairs.com/news04/2005/bankruptcy_study.html.

Meenan, Robert F. "Improving the Public's Health: Some Further Reflections." *New England Journal of Medicine*, January 1, 1976, pp. 45–46.

Mokdad, Ali H., et al. "Actual Causes of Death in the United States, 2000." *Journal of the American Medical Association*, vol. 291, no. 10; March 10, 2004. Available online. URL: http://jama.ama-assn.org/cgi/content/abstract/291/10/1238.

National Coalition on Health Care. "Health Insurance Costs: Facts on the Cost of Health Insurance and Health Care." Available online. URL: http://www.nchc.org/facts/cost.shtml.

Peikoff, Leonard. "Health Care Is Not a Right." Speech delivered December 1993, reprinted in *Capitalism*, January 23, 1998. Available online. URL: http://www.capmag.com/article.asp?ID=9.

Richman, Sheldon. "Perspective: The Right to Medical Care." *The Freeman*, September 1, 1997. Available online. URL: http://www.thefreemanonline.org/departments/perspective-the-right-to-medical-care/.

Schneiderman, Lawrence, M.D. "On Ethics and Medicine." *Healthwise*, University of California–San Diego, May 2001, pp. 4–5.

Thurow, Lester. "Learning to Say 'No.'" *New England Journal of Medicine*, vol. 311, no. 24, 1984, pp. 1569–1572.

U.S. Census Bureau. "Health Insurance Coverage Status and Type of Coverage by Sex, Race, and Hispanic Origin: 1999 to 2007." Available online. URL: http://www.census.gov/hhes/www/hlthins/historic/hihistt1.xls.

Wennberg, John E., and Elliot S. Fisher, et al. Dartmouth Atlas Project of Health Care. *The Care of Patients with Severe Chronic Illness: An Online Report on the Medicare Program*. Lebanon, N.H.: Trustees of Dartmouth College, 2006. Available online. URL: http://www.dartmouthatlas.org/press/2006_atlas_press_release.shtm.

Will, George W. "Freedom of Choice in Health Care." Townhall.com, October 27, 2008. Available online. URL: http://townhall.com/columnists/GeorgeWill/2008/10/27/freedom_of_choice_in_health_care.

Zinser, Lin, and Paul Hsieh. "Moral Health Care vs. 'Universal Health Care.'" *Objective Standard*, vol. 2, no. 4, Winter 2007. Available online. URL: http://www.theobjectivestandard.com/issues/2007-winter/moral-vs-universal-health-care.asp.

Web Sites

American Medical Association (AMA)

http://www.ama-assn.org
Web site of the nation's largest organization of medical doctors.

American Nurses Association (ANA)

http://www.ana.org
Web site of the nation's largest organization of professional nurses.

America's Health Insurance Plans (AHIP)

http://www.ahip.org/
National advocacy association for companies that offer health insurance.

Center for Economic and Social Rights (CESR)

http://www.cesr.org
The center works with national and international organizations to promote social justice through human rights. CESR believes universal healthcare is a right.

Centers for Medicare and Medicaid Services (CMS)

http://www.cms.hhs.gov/
This section of the U.S. Department of Health and Human Services administers the nation's largest publicly funded programs of health insurance for people over age 65 and the indigent, as well as SCHIP (the State Children's Health Insurance Program), which was launched in 1997.

Fraser Institute

http://www.fraserinstitute.org/
This nonprofit Canadian organization "measures and studies the impact of government interventions on individuals and society." They have published materials that criticize the single-payer healthcare program in Canada.

National Business Group on Health

http://www.businessgrouphealth.org/
This organization offers its corporate members business solutions as it "targets the key issues of health care costs, safety and quality."

New America Foundation

http://www.newamerica.net/
A nonprofit, nonpartisan public-policy institute that promotes new ideas to deal with the challenges facing the United States; the foundation supports universal healthcare coverage.

141

Physicians for a National Healthcare Plan

http://www.pnhp.org/

An organization of physicians who support a single-payer system of universal healthcare in the United States. The site contains articles, reports, statistics, and legislative updates.

Veterans Health Administration (VHA)

http://www1.va.gov/health/index.asp

A U.S. government Web site describing health services provided to veterans.

World Health Organization (WHO)

http://who.org

This organization directs and coordinates global health research, initiatives, and health programs within the United Nations system.

PICTURE CREDITS

PAGE

15: Newscom
59: Newscom
68: Newscom
100: AP Images

CONTRIBUTORS

VICTORIA SHERROW is a freelance writer and a member of the Society for Children's Book Writers. She is the author of many books for middle and high school readers, including *Great Scientists, Political Leaders and Peacemakers,* and several titles in the POINT/COUNTERPOINT series.

ALAN MARZILLI, M.A., J.D., lives in Birmingham, Ala., and is a program associate with Advocates for Human Potential, Inc., a research and consulting firm based in Sudbury, Mass., and Albany, N.Y. He primarily works on developing training and educational materials for agencies of the federal government on topics such as housing, mental health policy, employment, and transportation. He has spoken on mental health issues in 30 states, the District of Columbia, and Puerto Rico; his work has included training mental health administrators, nonprofit management and staff, and people with mental illnesses and their families on a wide variety of topics, including effective advocacy, community-based mental health services, and housing. He has written several handbooks and training curricula that are used nationally—as far away as the territory of Guam. He managed statewide and national mental health advocacy programs and worked for several public interest lobbying organizations while studying law at Georgetown University. He has written more than a dozen books, including numerous titles in the POINT/COUNTERPOINT series.